GENESIS:

A Closer
LOOK

GENESIS:

A CLOSER LOOK.

A
TRANSLITERATED VERSION
with
COMMENTARY
of the opening ten chapters of the
HOLY BIBLE

by

Mitch Kaminski

First Edition

TRUTH PUBLICATIONS

BOX 596 —— LOMBARD IL. —— 60148

Printed in the U.S.A.
by
TRI-STATE LITHO
Kingston, NY. 12401

ISBN: 0-9701646-0-2

Library of Congress 00-091865

Bringing Light

to a

World in Darkness

The fool hath said in his heart, there is no God. They are corrupt, they have done abominable works, there is none that doeth good.

(Ps. 14:1, 53:1)

Hear now this, O foolish people, and without understanding; which have eyes, and see not; which have ears, and hear not:

(Jer. 5:21, Ezek. 12:2, Matt. 13:13)

To revere the Lord is the beginning of wisdom: a good understanding have all they that do His commandments: his praise endureth forever.

(Ps. 111:10)

Then said Jesus to the Multitude which believed Him, If ye continue in my word, then are ye my disciples indeed; And ye shall know the truth, and the truth shall make you free.

(John 8:31, 32)

TABLE OF CONTENTS.

OTHER TRANSLATIONS.

DIRECTIONS AND EXPLANATIONS.

INTRODUCTION.

TABLE OF CONTENTS.

THE WHOLE PICTURE.

OTHER TRANSLATIONS

THE KING JAMES VERSION

TRANSLATED OUT OF THE ORIGINAL TONGUES
AND WITH PREVIOUS TRANSLATIONS
DILIGENTLY COMPARED AND REVISED

THE HOLY BIBLE-REVISED STANDARD VERSION

TRANSLATED FROM THE ORIGINAL TONGUES
BEING THE VERSION SET FORTH A.D. 1611
REVISED A.D. 1881-1885 AND A.D. 1901
COMPARED WITH THE MOST ANCIENT AUTHORITIES
AND REVISED A.D. 1952

TANAKH-THE HOLY SCRIPTURES

THE NEW JPS TRANSLATION ACCORDING
TO THE TRADITIONAL HEBREW TEXT

HOLY BIBLE-FROM THE ANCIENT EASTERN TEXT

GEORGE M. LAMSA'S TRANSLATION
FROM THE ARAMAIC OF THE PESHITTA

THE BIBLE

A NEW TRANSLATION
BY JAMES MOFFATT

DIRECTIONS AND EXPLANATIONS.

This is an explanation of the symbols and study
helpers used in this book. In chapter one,

(GR) = Greek

1254 = Strong's Exhaustive Concordance number
for the word it is above. All the words
are Hebrew unless noted with (GR).

St.#1-c
(THAT THEN WAS) = Words in parentheses can be
explained and better understood by turning
to Study#1-c

1961 v.2:7
BECAME   =   Again we have Strongs Concordance
number, but with a Chapter and Verse
number that will help you to better
understand this word.

(vain = tohuw)
(king of Tyrus = Lucifer, Satan.)
(heart = mind)
(foundation = overthrow)=These are words that
can be interchanged
for better understanding.

[heaven and earth destroyed by God.]
[has not happened yet.] = Words and sentences
in brackets are
personal comments
for better
understanding.

All script text is of the King James Version.

I hope you will enjoy reading this book,

and may God bless you and your family.

INTRODUCTION

Today we in the religious society are flooded with books and television programming with most of them focusing in on Bible prophecy. Don't get me wrong, I love Bible prophecy and to me it's very exciting and very important. I also believe we are living in the last days, and the 2nd coming of Jesus is at the door. But there is so much more to learn from our Bible before we can get a clear picture of why we are here and what the plan of God really is.

This is the reason for writing **GENESIS: A CLOSER LOOK**. Since these are the last days, we should know exactly what has taken place in the past and our Bibles should no longer be a mystery to us. We should know just about every thing that has happened and all that has been a mystery to the generations of the past. In *Dan. 12:4* it says, *But thou, O Daniel, shut up the words, and seal the book, even to the time of the end: many shall run to and fro, and knowledge shall be increased.* Here God is telling Daniel that his plan for mankind will not be understood until the time of the end. Even Daniel himself did not understand what he wrote down. In *Dan. 12:8* it says, *and I heard, but I understood not: then said I, O my Lord, what shall be the end of these things? 9) And he said, Go thy way, Daniel: for the words are closed up and sealed till the time of the end.* [which is now] *10) Many shall be purified, and made white, and tried; but the wicked shall do wickedly: and none of the wicked shall understand; but the wise shall understand.* [God's word]

Many Christians today have very little knowledge of God's word. It's rare that they even pick up a Bible. These Christians are considered to be on the so-called milk of the Bible. In *I Peter 2:2* it says, *As newborn babes, desire the sincere milk of the word, that ye may grow thereby*: Once you taste the truth of the Bible, your need for more grows. Many of today's preachers or evangelists only teach the milk of the Bible. This is because they need new members in their organization. They prey on newly converted Christians hoping in turn to get donations sent in. These ministries over and over continue in milk preaching never moving on to new truths and growing in the Spirit as we are supposed to do. Even though you are ready to grow spiritually, the process does take time. In *I COR. 3:2* it says, *I have fed you with milk, and not with meat: for hitherto ye were not able to bear it, neither yet now are ye able. 3) For ye are yet carnal: for whereas there is among you envying, and strife, and divisions, are ye not carnal, and walk as men?* As a person grows more and more hungry for the word of God, their mind and way of thinking changes. They start to shy away from the traditions of man.

They want and have a desire to walk in the way of the Lord. Many times, the now child of God, tends to seek a teacher who can help them to grow in the truth of God. *Isaiah 28:9* says, *Whom shall teach knowledge? and whom shall he make to understand doctrine?them that are weaned from the milk, and drawn from the breasts. 10) For precept must be upon precept, precept upon pre- cept; line upon line here a little, and there a little:* A good teacher of the word of God will always teach precept upon precept, line upon line. He will know where in the Bible certain truths can be documented or explained better. The whole idea is to let the Bible explain and prove itself. In the end, you will learn and know the truth of God's word.

God said that wisdom and knowledge will increase in the end times. In Rev. which means reveling, there is talk about a great famine. But what is this famine? The answer is in *Amos 8:11-13*. *11) Behold, the days come, saith the Lord God, that I will send a famine in the land, not a famine of bread, nor of thirst for water, but of HEARING THE WORDS OF THE LORD: 12) And they shall wander from sea to sea, and from north even to the east, they shall run to and fro to seek the WORD OF THE LORD, and shall not find it. 13) In that day shall the fair virgins and young men faint for thirst.* The end of the age famine is for understanding the word of God. [the Bible.]

God is pouring out His wisdom and knowledge to those who seek the truth about His word. There are some who don't even have a choice. [Moses, Paul, etc.] In *Eph.1:4* it says, *According as He hath chosen us, in Him BEFORE THE FOUNDATION* (overthrow) *of the world, that we should be holy and without blame before Him in love: 5) Having PREDESTINATED US unto the adoption of children by Jesus Christ to himself, according to the good pleasure of his WILL* (plan). Going on to verse *9) Having made known unto us the MYSTERY OF HIS WILL* (plan), *according to His good pleasure which He hath purposed in Himself: 10) That in the dispensation of the fulness of times he Might gather together in one all things in Christ, both which are in Heaven, and which are on Earth; even in Him: 11) In whom also we have obtained an inheritance, being PREDESTINATED according to the purpose of Him who worketh all things after the counsel of His own WILL* (plan)*: 12) That we should be to the praise of His glory, who first trusted in Christ.* Many times God chooses you; you DON'T choose God.

Learning truth will help you to understand life and will also help cope with the days' stresses and problems. Yahshua said in *John 17:16, They are not of the world,* [followers] *even as I am not of the world. 17) Sanctify them through thy truth: thy word is truth.* And in *John 8:31* Yahshua said, *If ye continue in my word, then are ye my* **DISCIPLES** (students) *indeed; 32) And ye shall know the truth, and* **THE TRUTH SHALL MAKE YOU FREE.** Knowing truth and God's overall plan really does set you free.

In this book **GENESIS: A CLOSER LOOK**, I will take you through chapters 1 to 10. You will read many things you never heard of before and will probably for the rest of your life, change some things you always thought were true.

KJV

1:1 In the beginning God created the heaven and the earth.
2 And the earth was without form, and void; and darkness was upon the face of the deep. And the spirit of God moved upon the face of the waters.

RSV

1:1 In the beginning God created the heavens and the earth.
2 The earth was without form and void, and darkness was upon the face of the deep; and the Spirit of God was moving over the face of the waters.

TANAKH

1:1 When God began to create heaven and earth-2 the earth being unformed and void, with darkness over the surface of the deep and a wind from God sweeping over the water

HOLY BIBLE-GML

1:1 God created the heavens and the earth in the very beginning.
2 And the earth was without form, and void; and darkness was upon the face of the deep. And the Spirit of God moved upon the face of the water.

HOLY BIBLE-JM

1:1 This is the story of how the universe was formed.
When God began to form the universe, 2 the world was void and vacant, darkness lay over the abyss; but the spirit of God was hovering over the waters.

GENESIS (GR) = Generation,Creation.

CHAPTER ONE

1:1   1254
   In the beginning God   **CREATED**   the
                  SS.#1-c

Heavens and the Earth; **THAT THEN WAS,**

complete and perfect.

1) 1254
   bara
   to produce
   something
   new.

1:2
   But because of the rebellion of

Lucifer, the Heavens and Earth;
           1961 v.2:7   922
THAT THEN WAS,   **BECAME**   **VOID**
   8414
WITHOUT FORM, and darkness covered

the face of the deep. And the Holy

Spirit of God moved upon the face

of the waters.

1) 1961
   hayah
   to become

2) 922
   bohuw
   to be empty,
   vacant, ruins.

3) 8414
   tohuw
   to lie waste,
   wilderness,
   vain.

* *

SCRIPTURE STUDY #1
GENESIS 1:1,2

A) Job 38:4-12
B) Prov. 8:22-30
C) II Peter 3:5-9
D) Isaiah 45:18   (vain = tohuw)
E) Jer. 4::22-28   [heaven and earth destroyed by God.]
                  v.25 there was no man.
                  this is not Noah's flood.
F) Ezek. 28:12-19   (king of Tyrus = Lucifer,Satan.)
                  (covering = protector)
G) Isaiah 14:12-17
H) Ezek. 28:1-10   (king of Tyrus = Satan)
                  (heart = mind)
I) Matt. 13:35   (foundation = overthrow)
J) Rev. 12:7-9   [has not happened yet.]

VERY IMPORTANT THAT YOU READ ALL THE
SCRIPTURES THAT ARE ABOVE.

KJV

3 And God said, Let there be light: and there was light. 4 And God saw the light, that it was good: and God divided the light from the darkness. 5 And God called the light day, and the darkness he called Night. And the evening and the morning were the first day. 6 And God said, Let there be a firmament in the midst of the waters, and let it divide the waters from the waters.
7 And God made the firmament, and divided the waters which were under the firmament from the waters which were above the firmament: and it was so.
8 And God called the firmament Heaven. And the evening and the morning were the second day.

RSV

3 And God said, "Let there be light"; and there was light. 4 And God saw that the light was good; and God separated the light from the darkness. 5 God called the light Day, and the darkness he called Night. And there was evening and there was morning, one day. 6 And God said, "Let there be a firmament in the midst of the waters, and let it separate the waters from the waters." 7 And God made the firmament and separated the waters which were under the firmament from the waters which were above the firmament. And it was so. 8 And God called the firmament Heaven. And there was evening and there was morning, a second day.

TANAKH

3 God said, "Let there be light"; and there was light. 4 God saw that the light was good, and God separated the light from the darkness. 5 God called the light Day, and the darkness He called Night. And there was evening and there was morning, a first day. 6 God said, "Let there be an expanse in the midst of the water, that it my separate water from water." 7 God made the expanse, and it separated the water which was below the expanse from the water which was above the expanse,. And it was so. 8 God called the expanse Sky. And there was evening and there was morning, a second day.

HOLY BIBLE-GML

3 And God said, Let there be light; and there was light. 4 And God saw the that the light was good; and God separated the light from the darkness. 5 And God called the light Day, and the darkness he called Night. And there was evening and there was morning, the first day. 6 And God said, Let there be a firmament in the midst of the waters, and let it divide the waters from the waters. 7 And God made the firmament, and divided the waters that were under the firmament from the waters that were above. the firmament; and it was so. 8 And God called the firmament Sky. And there was evening and there was morning, the second day.

HOLY BIBLE-JM

3 God said, "Let there be light," and there was light. 4 God saw that the light was good, and he separated the light from the darkness. 5 God called the light Day and the darkness he called Night. Evening came and morning came, making one day. 6 Then God said, "Let there be a Vault between the waters, to divide them"; 7 so God made the Vault, dividing the waters under the Vault from the waters above the Vault, 8 and God called the Vault heaven. Evening came and morning came, making the second day.

1:3
   And with all His glory, God said,

v.2:7
"Let there be light," and there BECAME

light.

1:4
   And God saw the light, and it was

beautiful. And God divided the light

from the darkness.

1:5
   And God called the light day, and

the darkness He called night. And the

evening and the morning was day one.

1:6
   And with all His glory, God said,

"Let there be an EXPANSE between the

waters. And let it divide the

v.10
WATERS OF EARTH from the

v.8
WATERS OF HEAVEN.

1:7
   And God divided the waters, and it

was done.

1:8
   And God called the waters of heaven

7549
the **FIRMAMENT**. And the evening and the

morning was day two.

NOTE:
v.3 starts with
the creation of
the Heavens and
Earth;
WHICH ARE NOW,
as written in
II Peter 3:7.

1) 7549
   raqiya
   a dome or arch
   of water.

4

9 And God said, Let the waters under the heaven be gathered together unto one place, and let the dry land appear: and it was so. 10 And God called the dry land Earth; and the gathering together of the waters called he Seas: and God saw that it was good. 11 And God said, Let the earth bring forth grass, the herb yielding seed, and the fruit tree yielding fruit after his kind, whose seed is in itself, upon the earth: and it was so.12 And the earth brought forth grass, and herb yielding seed after his kind, and the tree yielding fruit, whose seed was in itself, after his kind: and God saw that it was good. 13 And the evening and the morning were the third day.

9 And God said, "Let the waters under the heavens be gathered together into one place, and let the dry land appear." And it was so. 10 God called the dry land Earth, and the waters that were gathered together he called Seas. And God saw that it was good. 11 And God said, "Let the earth put forth vegetation, plants yielding seed, and fruit trees bearing fruit in their seed, eachaccording to its kind, upon the earth." And it was so. 12 The earth brought forth vegetation, plants yielding seed according to their own kinds, and trees bearing fruit in which is their seed, each according to its kind. And God saw that it was good. 13 And there was evening and there was morning, a third day.

9 God said, "Let the water below the sky be gathered into one area, that the dry land my appear." And it was so. 10 God called the dry land Earth, and the gathering of waters He called Seas. And God saw that this was good. 11 And God said, "Let the earth sprout vegetation: seed-bearing plants, fruit trees of every kind on earth that bear fruit with the seed in it." And it was so. 12 The earth brought forth vegetation: seed-bearing plants of every kind, and trees of every kind bearing fruit with the seed in it. And God saw that this was good. 13 And there was evening and there was morning, a third day.

9 And God said, "Let the waters that are under the sky be gathered together in one place, and let dry land appear; and it was so. 10 And God called the dry land Earth; and the gathering together of the waters he called Seas; and God saw that it was good. 11 And God said, Let the earth bring forth vegetation, the herb yielding seed after its kind, and the fruit tree yielding fruit after its kind, wherein is their seed, upon the earth; and it was so. 12 And the earth brought forth vegetation, the herb yielding seed after its kind, and the tree bearing fruit, wherein is its seed, after its kind; and God saw that it was good. 13 And there was evening and there was morning, the third day.

9 Then God said, "Let the waters below heaven be gathered into one place, to let dry land appear." And so it was. 10 God called the dry land Earth, and the gathered waters he called Seas. God saw that it was good. 11 And God said, "Let the earth put out verdure, plants that bear seed and trees yielding fruit of every kind, fruit with seed in it." 12 And so it was; the earth brought forth verdure, plants bearing seed of every kind and trees yielding fruit of every kind, fruit with seed in it. God saw that it good. 13 Evening came and morning came, making the third day.

1:9
 And with all His glory,

God said,"Let the waters under the
 v.6
EXPANSE be gathered together unto one

place. And let dry land appear."

And it was done.

1:10
 And God called the dry land Earth.

And the waters that gathered together,

He called Seas. And God saw that it

was beautiful.

1:11
 And again with all His glory,

God said,"Let the Earth bring forth

grass; that's yielding seed, and

trees; that yield fruit, and whose

seeds are in itself, and multiplies

after it's own kind."

1:12
 And so on the Earth was brought

forth all types of plants, trees, and

vegetation. All yielding seed within

itself and multiplying after it's own

kind. And God saw that it was beautiful.

1:13
 And the evening and the morning was

day three.

14 And God said, Let there be lights in the firmament of the heaven to divide the day from the night; and let them be for signs, and for seasons, and for days, and years: 15 And let them be for lights in the firmament of the heaven to give light upon the earth: and it was so. 16 And God made two great lights; the greater one to rule the day, and the lesser light to rule the night: he made the stars also. 17 And God set them in the firmament of heaven to give light upon the earth, 18 And to rule over the day and over the night, and to divide the light from the darkness: and God saw that it was good. 19 And the evening and the morning were the fourth day.

14 And God said, "Let there be lights in the firmament of the heavens to separate the day from the night; and let them be for signs and for seasons and for days and years, 15 and let them be lights in the firmament of the heavens to give light upon the earth." And it was so. 16 And God made two great lights, the greater light to rule the day, and the lesser one to rule the night; he made the stars also. 17 And God set them in the firmament of the heavens to give light upon the earth, 18 to rule over the day and over the night, and to separate the light from the darkness. And God saw that it was good. 19 And there was evening and there was morning, a fourth day.

14 God said, "Let there be lights in the expanse of the sky to separate day from night; they shall serve as signs for the set times – the days and the years; 15 and they shall serve as lights in the expanse of the sky to shine upon the earth." And it was so. 16 God made the two great lights, the greater light to dominate the day and the lesser light to dominate the night, and the stars. 17 And God set them in the expanse of the sky to shine upon the earth, 18 to dominate the day and the night, and to separate light from darkness. And God saw that this was good. 19 And there was evening and there was morning, a fourth day.

14 Then God said, Let there be lights in the firmament of heaven to separate the day from the night; and let them be for signs, and for seasons, and for days, and years. 15 And let them be for lights in the firmament of the heaven to give light upon the earth; and it was so. 16 And God made two great lights, the greater light to rule the day, and the smaller light to rule the night; and the stars also. 17 And God set them in the firmament of the heavens to give light upon the earth, 18 And to rule over the day and over the night, and to separate the light from the darkness; and God saw that it was good. 19 And there was evening and there was morning, the fourth day.

14 Then God said, "Let there be lights in the Vault of heaven to separate day from night, to mark out the sacred seasons, the days and the years; 15 let them shine in the Vault of heaven, to shed light on the earth"; and so it was. 16 For God made the two great lights, the greater light to rule the day, the lesser light together with the stars to rule the night; 17 God set them in the Vault of heaven to shed light upon earth, 18 to rule the day and the night, and to separate light and darkness. And God saw that it was good. 19 Evening came and morning came, making the fourth day.

1:14
    And with all His glory,
                                   v.16
God said,"Let there be **LUMINARIES** set in
        v.8
the **FIRMAMENT** of Heaven to divide the day

from the night: and let them be for signs,

and for seasons, and for days and years.

1:15
    And let the lights illuminate through
        v.8
the **FIRMAMENT** of Heaven to give light

upon the Earth." And it was done.

1:16   6213
    And with all His glory, God **MADE** the

two great Luminaries; the greater one to
        (sun)
rule the **DAY**. And the lesser one to rule
     (moon)
the **NIGHT**. And all the stars of the

Heavens He also made.

1:17   v.8
    And God set them in the **FIRMAMENT** of

Heaven to give light upon the Earth,

1:18
    And to rule over the day and over

the night, and to divide the light from

the darkness: and God saw that it was

beautiful.

1:19
    And the evening and the morning was

day four.

1) 6213
   rasah
   to produce
   by miracle.

8

KJV

20 And God said, Let the waters bring forth abundantly the moving creature that hath life, and fowl that may fly above the earth in the open firmament of heaven. 21 And God created great whales, and every living creature that moveth, which the waters brought forth abundantly, after their kind, and every winged fowl after his kind: and God saw that it was good. 22 And God blessed them, saying, Be fruitful, and multiply, and fill the waters in the seas, and let the fowl multiply in the earth. 23 And the evening and the morning were the fifth day. 24 And God said, Let the earth bring forth the living creatures after his kind, cattle, and creeping thing, and the beast of the earth after his kind: and it was so.

RSV

20 And God said, "Let the waters bring fourth swarms of living creatures, and let birds fly above the earth across the firmament of the heavens." 21 So God created the great sea monsters and every living creature that moves, with which the waters swarm, according to their kinds, and every winged bird according to its kind. And God saw that it was good. 22 And God blessed them, saying, "Be fruitful and multiply and fill the waters in the seas, and let birds multiply on the earth." 23 And there was evening and there was morning, a fifth day. 24 And God said, "Let the earth bring fourth living creatures according to their kinds: cattle and creeping things and beasts of the earth according to their kinds." And it was so.

TANAKH

20 God said, "Let the waters bring forth swarms of living creatures, and birds that fly above the earth across the expanse of the sky." 21 God created the great sea monsters, and all the living creatures of every kind that creep, which the waters brought forth in swarms, and all the winged birds of every kind. And God saw that this was good. 22 God blessed them saying, "Be fertile and increase, fill the waters in the seas, and let the birds increase on the earth." 23 And there was evening and there was morning, a fifth day. 24 God said, "Let the earth bring forth every kind of living creature: cattle, creeping things, and wild beasts of every kind." And it was so.

HOLY BIBLE-GML

20 And God said, Let the waters bring forth swarms of living creatures, and let fowl fly above the earth in the open firmament of the heaven. 21 And God created great sea monsters, and every living creature that moves, which the waters brought forth abundantly after their kind, and every winged fowl after its kind; and God saw that it was good. 22 And God blessed them, saying, Be fruitful and multiply, and fill the waters in the seas, and let fowl multiply on the earth. 23 And there was evening and there was morning, the fifth day. 24 Then God said, Let the earth bring forth living creatures after their kind, cattle, and creeping things, and beasts of the earth after their kind; and it was so.

HOLY BIBLE- JM

20 Then God said, "Let the waters teem with shoals of living creatures, and let birds fly over the earth under the open Vault of heaven." 21 So God formed the great sea-monsters and every kind of living creature that moves, with which the waters teem, and also every kind of winged bird. 22 God saw that it was good, and God blessed them; "be fruitful," he said, "multiply, and fill the waters of the sea; let the birds multiply on earth." 23 Evening came and morning came, making the fifth day. 24 Then God said, "Let the earth bring forth every kind of living creature, animals, reptiles, and wild beasts." And so it was.

1:20
    And with all His glory,

God said,"Let the waters be filled

abundantly with moving creatures that
          (soul=body) 5315
have   **LIFE.**   And birds that may
                v.6
fly above the Earth in the **EXPANSE.**

1:21   v.1
    And with all His glory, God **CREATED**
    (soul) v.20
every **CREATURE** that moved in the seas;

all multiplying after their own kind.

And God created all the birds, and they

also multiplied after their own kind.

1:22
    And God blessed them saying,

"Be fruitful and multiply, and fill the

waters in the seas, and let the birds

multiply and fill the skies."

1:23
    And the evening and the morning

was day five.

1:24
    And with all His glory, God said,

"Let the Earth be filled abundantly

with living creatures, all multiplying

 after their own kind."

1) 5315
nephesh
any life form
which lives and
breathes on the
Earth.

25 And God made the beasts of the earth after his kind, and cattle after their kind, and every thing that creepeth upon the earth after his kind: and God saw that it was good. 26 And God said, Let us make man in our image, after our likeness: and let them have dominion over the fish of the sea, and over the fowl of the air, and over the cattle, and over all the earth, and over every creeping thing that creepeth upon the earth. 27 So God created man in his own image, in the image of God created he him; male and female created he them. 28 And God blessed them, and God said unto them, Be fruitful, and multiply, and replenish the earth, and subdue it: and have dominion over the fish of the sea, and over the fowl of the air, and over every living thing that moveth upon the earth.

25 and God made the beasts of the earth according to their kinds and the cattle according to their kinds, and everything that creeps upon the ground according to its kind. And God saw that it was good. 26 Then God said, "Let us make man in our image, after our likeness; and let them have dominion over the fish of the sea, and over the birds of the air, and over the cattle, and over all the earth, and over every creeping thing that creeps upon the earth." 27 So God created man in his own image, in the image of God he created him; male and female he created them. 28 And God blessed them, and God said to them, "Be fruitful and multiply, and fill the earth and subdue it; and have dominion over the fish of the sea and over the birds of the air and over every living thing that moves upon the earth."

25 God made wild beasts of every kind and cattle of every kind, and all kinds of creeping things of the earth. And God saw that this was good. 26 And God said, "Let us make man in our image, after our likeness. They shall rule the fish of the sea, and the birds of the sky, the cattle, the whole earth, and all the creeping things that creep on earth." 27 And God created man in His image, in the image of God He created him; male and female He created them. 28 God blessed them and God said to them, "Be fertile and increase, fill the earth and master it; and rule the fish of the sea, the birds of the sky, and all the living things that creep on earth.

25 And God made the beasts of the earth after their kind, and the cattle after their kind, and everything that creeps upon the earth after its kind; and God saw that it was good. 26 Then God said, Let us make man in our image, after our likeness; and let them have dominion over the fish of the sea, and over the fowl of the air, and over the cattle, and over all the wild beasts of the earth, and over every creeping thing that creeps upon the earth. 27 So God created man in his own image, in the image of God he created him; male and female he created them. 28 And God blessed them, and God said to them, Be fruitful, and multiply, and fill the earth, and subdue it; and have dominion over the fish of the sea, and over the fowl of the air, and over the cattle, and over all the wild beasts that move upon the earth.

25 God made every kind of wild beast, every kind of animal, and every kind of reptile; and God saw that it was good. 26 Then said God, "Let us make man in our own likeness, to resemble us, with mastery over the fish in the sea, the birds of the air, the animals, every wild beast of the earth, and every reptile that crawls on the earth." 27 So God formed man in his own likeness, in the likeness of God he formed him, male and female he formed both. 28 And God blessed them; God said to them, "Be fruitful, multiply, fill the earth and subdue it, mastering the fish in the sea, the birds of the air, and every living creature that crawls on the earth."

1:25

And God made all the beasts, cattle, birds, and reptiles, and all the other life forms that exist on the Earth.

And all that God made multiplyed after it's own kind.

1:26

And with all His glory,

(mankind)=120

God said,"Let us make **MAN** in our

(shape,form)   (unfallen state = sinless)

IMAGE, and in our **LIKENESS**.

And let them have dominion over the fish, and the birds, and all the beasts, cattle, reptiles, and every living life form that exist upon the Earth."

1:27   v.1   v.26

So God **CREATED** **MAN** in His form.

v.26

In the form of God, **MAN** was created.

Both **MALE AND FEMALE** of every race that mankind has, God created.

1:28

And with all His glory,

God blessed **THEM ALL** and said to **THEM,**

"Be fruitful and multiply, and **FILL AGAIN** the Earth. And subdue it, and have dominion over the fish, birds, beasts, cattle, reptiles, and all life forms of the Earth."

1) 120
adam
all the differant
races of mankind
created at this
time except one.
see v.2:7

KJV

29 And God said, Behold, I have given you every herb bearing seed, which is upon the face of all the earth, and every tree, in the which is the fruit of a tree yielding seed; to you it shall be for meat. 30 And to every beast of the earth, and to every fowl of the air, and to every thing that creepeth upon the earth, wherein there is life, I have given every green herb for meat: and it was so. 31 And God saw every thing that he had made, and, behold, it was very good. And the evening and the morning were the sixth day. 2:1 Thus the heavens and the earth were finished, and all the host of them.

RSV

29 And God said, "Behold, I have given you every plant yielding seed which is upon the face of all the earth, and every tree with seed in its fruit; you shall have them for food. 30 And to every beast of the earth, and to every bird of the air, and to everything that creeps on the earth, everything that has the breath of life, I have given every green plant for food." And it was so. 31 And God saw everything that he had made, and behold, it was very good. And there was evening and there was morning, a sixth day. 2:1 Thus the heavens and the earth were finished, and all the host of them.

TANAKH

29 God said, "See, I give you every seed-bearing plant that is upon all the earth, and every tree that has seed-bearing fruit; they shall be yours for food. 30 And to all the animals on land, to all birds of the sky, and to everything that creeps on earth, in which there is the breath of life, [I give] all the green plants for food." And it was so. 31 And God saw all that He had made, and found it very good. And there was evening and there was morning, the sixth day. 2:1 The heaven and earth was finished, and all their array.

HOLY BIBLE-GML

29 And God said, Behold, I have given you every herb yielding seed, which is upon the face of all the earth, and every tree which bears fruit yielding seed; to you it shall be for food. 30 And to every beast of the earth, and to every fowl of the air, and to every thing that creeps upon the earth, wherein there is life, I have given every green herb for food; and it was so. 31 And God saw everything that he had made, and behold, it was very good. And there was evening and there was morning, the sixth day. 2:1 Thus the heavens and the earth were finished, and all the host of them.

HOLY BIBLE-JM

29 God also said, "See, I give you every plant that bears seed all over the earth, and every tree with seed in its fruit; be that your food. 30 To every wild beast on earth, to every bird of the air, and to every living creature that crawls on earth, I give all the green growth for food." And so it was. 31 God saw all that he had made, and very good it was. Evening came and morning came, making the sixth day. 2:1 Thus was the universe and its array all finished.

1:29
    And God said,"Behold I have given
you all the plants, herbs, trees, and
vegetation; yielding it's seed, bringing
forth fruit, and multiplying after it's
own kind, for you to eat.

1:30
    And to all the beast of the Earth,
and to every bird of the air, and to
every thing that creeps upon the Earth;
which is a living, breathing ^{v.20} **SOUL**,
to them I also give every plant and tree
for food." And it was done.

1:31
    And God saw everything that He had
made, and behold it was **VERY BEAUTIFUL**.
And the evening and the morning was
THE SIXTH DAY.

CHAPTER TWO
2:1
    And so, the Heavens and Earth;
    SS.#1-c
WHICH ARE NOW were finished.
        (angels = spirit beings)
And all the **CHILDREN** of God were now
prepared and waiting to go through this;
FLESH AND BLOOD second world age.

NOTE:
First time THE is
used in the front
of the word DAY

14

2 And on the seventh day God ended his work which he had made, and he rested on the seventh day from all his work which he had made. 3 And God blessed the seventh day, and sanctified it: because that in it he had rested from all his work which God created and made. 4 These are the generations of the heavens and of the earth when they were created, in the day that the Lord God made the earth and the heavens, 5 And every plant of the field before it was in the earth, and every herb of the field before it grew: for the Lord God had not caused it to rain upon the earth, and there was not a man to till the ground. 6 But there went up a mist from the earth, and watered the whole face of the ground.

2 And on the seventh day God finished his work which he had done, and he rested on the seventh day from all his work which he had done. 3 So God blessed the seventh day and hallowed it, because on it God rested from all his work which he had done in creation. 4 These are the generations of the heavens and the earth when they were created. In the day that the Lord God made the earth and the heavens, 5 when no plant of the field was yet in the earth and no herb of the field had yet sprung up- for the Lord God had not caused it to rain upon the earth, and there was no man to till the ground; 6 but a mist went up from the earth and watered the whole face of the ground-

2 On the seventh day God finished the work that He had been doing, and He ceased on the seventh day from all the work that He had done. 3 And God blessed the seventh day and declared it holy, because on it God ceased from all the work of creation that He had done. 4 Such is the story of heaven and earth when they were created. When the Lord God made earth and heaven—5 when no shrub of the field was yet on earth and no grasses of the field had yet sprouted, because the Lord God had not sent rain upon the earth and there was no man to till the soil, 6 but a flow would well up from the ground and water the whole surface of the earth—

2 And on the sixth day God finished his works which he had made, and he rested on the seventh day from all his works which he had made. 3 So God blessed the seventh day, and sanctified it; because in it he had rested from all his works which God created and made. 4 These are the generations of the heavens and of the earth when they were created, in the day that the Lord God made the heavens and the earth. 5 And all the trees of the field were not yet in the ground, and every herb of the field had not yet sprung up; for the Lord God had not yet caused it to rain upon the earth, and watered all the face of the ground. 6 But a powerful spring gushed out of the earth, and watered all the face of the ground.

2 On the seventh day God ceased his work, he desisted from working on the seventh day; 3 so God blessed and consecrated the seventh day, because on it he desisted from all his work of creation. 4 at the time when God the Eternal made the earth and heaven, 5 there was as yet no shrub on earth, and no plant had sprung up; for God the Eternal had not sent rain on earth, and there was no one to till the soil—though a mist used to rise from the earth and watered all the surface of the ground.

2:2
And on the sixth day, God stoped all
his work. And on day seven, God observed
and watched over all His achievement.

2:3
And God blessed the seventh day and
made it holy, because that in that day
God had stopped from all His work.

2:4
And so that was the history of
the Heavens and Earth; **THAT ARE NOW**,
and in the order that it was all created.

2:5
Now every plant, herb, and tree grew
even though the Lord God had not caused
water to rain down upon the Earth, but
there did come up from the ground; mist,
fog, and a morning dew. And that's how
the whole face of the Earth was watered.

2:6
Now the Lord God had on the Earth,
Fishermen and Hunters, but there was
no man to **TILL** (work) the ground. The Earth
did not have a Farmer.

NOTE:
#7-
Spiritual
perfection,
Spiritual
compleatness.

16

KJV

7 And the Lord God formed man of the dust of the ground, and breathed into his nostrils the breath of life; and man became a living soul. 8 And the Lord God planted a garden eastward in Eden; and there he put the man whom he had formed. 9 And out of the ground made the Lord God to grow every tree that is pleasant to the sight, and good for food; the tree of life also in the midst of the garden, and the tree of knowledge of good and evil.

RSV

7 Then the Lord God formed man of the dust of the ground, and breathed into his nostrils the breath of life; and the man became a living being. 8 And the Lord God planted a garden in Eden, in the east; and there he put the man whom he had formed. 9 And out of the ground the Lord God made to grow every tree that is pleasant to the sight and good for food, the tree of life also in the midst of the garden, and the tree of the knowledge of good and evil.

TANAKH

7 the Lord God formed man from the dust of the earth. He blew into his nostrils the breath of life, and man became a living being. 8 The Lord God planted a garden in Eden, in the east, and placed there the man whom He had formed. 9 And from the ground the Lord God caused to grow every tree that was pleasing to the sight and good for food, with the tree of life in the middle of the garden, and the tree of knowledge of good and bad.

HOLY BIBLE-GML

7 And the Lord God formed Adam out of the soil of the earth, and breathed into his nostrils the breath of life; and man became a living being. 8 And the Lord God planted a garden eastward in Eden; and there he put the man whom he had formed. 9 And out of the ground the Lord God made to grow every tree that is pleasant to the sight and good for food; the tree of life also in the midst of the garden, and the tree of the knowledge of good and evil.

HOLY BIBLE-JM

7 Then the God Eternal moulded man from the dust of the ground, breathing into his nostrils the breath of life; this was how man became a living being. 8 In the land of Eden, to the far east, God the Eternal then planted a park, where he put the man whom he had moulded. 9 And from the ground God the Eternal made all sorts of trees to grow that were delightful to see and good to eat, with the tree of life and the tree that yields knowledge of good and evil in the centre of the park. 10 From Eden a river flowed to water the park, which on leaving the park branched into four streams; 11 the name of the first is Pison (the one which flows all round the land of Havilah, where there is gold—fine gold in that land!—with pearls and beryls), 13 the name of the second is Gihon (the one which flows all round the land of Ethiopia), 14 the name of the third is Hiddekel (the one which flows west of Assyria), and the fourth river is the Euphrates. 15 God the Eternal took man and put him in the park of Eden, to till it and to guard it.

2:7

So on the eighth day, the Lord God
3335   121
FORMED; like a potter, a **MAN** from the

dust of the ground; and breathed into
(Adam)=121
his nostrils; **LIFE.** And the **MAN**
1961   v.1:20
BECAME a **LIVING SOUL.**

2:8

And the Lord God made separately;

in the eastern quarter outside of Eden,

a **GARDEN PARADISE.** And there He put Adam;
v.7   v.7
the **MAN** who God **FORMED** from the dust of

the Earth.

2:9

And the Lord God made to grow, out of

the ground, every tree that is pleasant

to the eye, and good for food. And the

Lord God also put in the midst of the
(Jesus = Yahshua)
garden, the **TREE OF LIFE,** and the
·(Lucifer = Satan)
TREE with the **KNOWLEDGE OF GOOD AND EVIL.**

* *

1) 3335
   yatsar
   not like v.1:1
   or created #1254
   or made #6213

2) 121
   ha adham
   the man named
   Adam.
   (Adamic race)

3) 1961
   hayah
   this is the same
   word used in
   v.1:2, 1:3

SCRIPTURE STUDY #2
TREES=MEN/PEOPLE #6086, 6095, 6096

A) Mark 8:24
B) Isaiah 61:3
C) Matt. 7:15-20   (fruits = what they produce,accomplish,)
D) Matt. 12:33   (their work, offspring.)
E) Judges 9:7-15   (trees = people)
                        (promoted = king)
                        (Cedars of Lebanon = People of God)
F) Ezek. 31   (Assyrian = Satan)
                        (trees = men)
G) Hosea 14:4-9   I) Matt. 3:10   K) Rev. 2:7   M) John 6:25-65
H) Luke 3:9   J) Isaiah 14:8   L) Rev. 22:2

[Yahshua is the tree of LIFE, partake of His fruits.]

18

10 And a river went out of Eden to water the garden; and from thence it was parted, and became into four heads. 11 The name of the first is Pison: that is it which compasseth the whole land of Havilah, where there is gold; 12 And the gold of that land is good: there is bdellium and the onyx stone. 13 And the name of the second river is Gihon: the same is it that compasseth the whole land of Ethiopia. 14 And the name of the third river is Hiddekel: that is it which goeth toward the east of Assyria. And the fourth river is Euphrates. 15 And the Lord God took the man, and put him into the garden of Eden to dress it and to keep it. 16 And the Lord God commanded the man, saying, Of every tree of the garden thou mayest freely eat: 17 But of the tree of the knowledge of good and evil, thou shalt not eat of it: for in the day that thou eatest thereof thou shalt surely die.

10 A river flowed out of Eden to water the garden, and there it divided and became four rivers. 11 The name of the first is Pishon; it is the one which flows around the whole land of Havilah, where there is gold; 12 and the gold of that land is good; bdellium and onyx stones are there. 13 The name of the second river is Gihon, it is the one which flows around the whole land of Cush. 14 And the name of the third river is Tigris, which flows east of Assyria. And the fourth river is the Euphrates. 15 The Lord God took the man and put him in the garden of Eden to till it and keep it. 16 And the Lord God commanded the man, saying, "You may freely eat of every tree of the garden; 17 but of the tree of the knowledge of good and evil you shall not eat, for in the day that you eat of it you shall die."

10 A river issues from Eden to water the garden, and it then divides and becomes four branches. 11 The name of the first is Pishon, the one that winds through the whole land of Havilah, where the gold is. (12 The gold of that land is good; bdellium is there, and lapis lazuli.) 13 The name of the second river is Gihon, the one that winds through the whole land of Cush. 14 The name of the third river is Tigris, the one that flows east of Asshur. And the fourth river is the Euphrates. 15 The Lord God took the man and placed him in the garden of Eden, to till it and tend it. 16 And the Lord God commanded the man, saying, "Of every tree of the garden you are free to eat; 17 but as for the tree of knowledge of good and bad, you must not eat of it; for as soon as you eat of it, you shall die."

10 And a river flowed out of Eden to water the garden; and from thence it divided and became into four heads. 11 The name of the first is Pishon; it is the one which encircles the whole land of Havilah, where there is gold; 12 And the gold of that land is good; there is also beryllium and the onyx stone. 13 And the name of the second river is Gihon, the one which encircles the whole land of Ethiopia. 14 And the name of the third river is Deklat (Tigris); it is the one which flows east of Assyria. And the fourth river is the Euphrates. 15 And the Lord God took the man, and put him in the garden of Eden to till it and to keep it. 16 And the Lord God commanded the man, saying, Of every tree of the garden you may freely eat; 17 But of the tree of the knowledge of good and evil, you shall not eat; for in the day that you eat of it you shall surely die.

2:10
    And a river flowed out of Eden to
              v.8
water the **GARDEN PARADISE,** and from

there it parted into four separate

rivers.

2:11
    The name of the first is Pison,

which encircled the land of Havilah.

2:12
    And the gold of that land is good;

there is bdellium and the onyx stone.

2:13
    And the name of the second river

is Gihon, which is east of the Tigris;

the third river.

2:14
    And the name of the fourth river

is Euphrates, or the great river.

2:15
    And the Lord God took Adam, and

put him into the garden, to cultivate

it, and to preserve it.

2:16
    And the Lord God commanded Adam,

saying, "Of every **TREE** of the garden,

you may freely partake of.

2:17
    But of the **TREE** with the knowledge
              v.3:3
of good and evil, you shall not **TOUCH**

or partake of it, because in   **THE DAY**
        (partake)   SS.#2-c,d
that you **EAT** of his **FRUIT,** you

shall surely die."

NOTE:
    THE DAY
II Peter 3:8
Beloved, be not ignorant
of this one thing, that
one day is with he Lord
as a thousand years, and
a thousand years as one
day.

Genesis 5:5
And all the days that
Adam lived were nine
hundred and thirty
years: and he died.

COMMENT:
Adam partook of
(ss.#2-c,d)
SATAN'S FRUIT, and as
God said, "In that day
you shall surely die."
Adam did not last one
day with the Lord.

18 And the Lord God said, It is not good that the man should be alone; I will make him an help meet for him. 19 And out of the ground the Lord God formed every beast of the field, and every fowl of the air; and brought them unto Adam to see what he would call them: and whatsoever Adam called every living creature, that was the name thereof. 20 And Adam gave names to all cattle, and to the fowl of the air, and to every beast of the field; but for Adam there was not found an help meet for him. 21 And the Lord God caused a deep sleep to fall upon Adam, and he slept: and he took one of his ribs, and closed up the flesh instead thereof; 22 And the rib, which the Lord God had taken from man, made he a woman, and brought her unto the man. 23 And Adam said, This is now bone of my bones,· and flesh of my flesh: she shall be called Woman, because she was taken out of Man.

RSV

18 Then the Lord God said, "It is not good that the man should be alone; I will make him a helper fit for him." 19 So out of the ground the Lord God formed every beast of the field and every bird of the air, and brought them to the man to see what he would call them; and whatever the man called every living creature, that was its name. 20 The man gave names to all cattle, and to the birds of the air, and to every beast of the field; but for the man there was not found a helper fit for him. 21 So the Lord God caused a deep sleep to fall upon the man, and while he slept took one of his ribs and closed up its place with flesh; 22 and the rib which the Lord God had taken from the man he made into a woman and brought her to the man. 23 Then the man said, "This at last is bone of my bones and flesh of my flesh; she shall be called Woman, because she was taken out of man."

TANAKH

18 The Lord God said, "It is not good for man to be alone; I will make a fitting helper for him." 19 And the Lord God formed out of the earth all the wild beasts and all the birds of the sky, and brought them to the man to see what he would call them; and whatever the man called each living creature, that would be its name. 20 And the man gave names to all the cattle and to the birds of the sky and to all the wild beasts; but for Adam no fitting helper was found. 21 So the Lord God cast a deep sleep upon the man; and, while he slept, He took one of his ribs and closed up the flesh at that spot. 22 And the Lord God fashioned the rib that He had taken from the man into a woman; and He brought her to the man. 23 Then the man said, "This one at last Is bone of my bones And flesh of my flesh. This one shall be called Woman, For from man was she taken.

HOLY BIBLE-GNL

18 Then the Lord God said, It is not good that the man should be alone; I will make him a helper who is like him. 19 And out of the ground the Lord God formed every beast of the field, and every fowl of the air; and brought them to Adam to see what he would call them; and whatever Adam called every living creature, that was its name. 20 And Adam gave names to all the cattle, and to all fowl of the air, and to all wild beasts; but for Adam there was not found a helper who was equal to him. 21 So the Lord God caused a deep sleep to fall upon Adam, and he slept; and He took one of his ribs, and closed up the place with flesh in its stead; 22 And of the rib which the Lord God had taken from Adam He made a woman, and brought her to Adam. 23 And Adam said, This is now bone of my bones, and flesh of my flesh; she shall be called Woman, because she was taken out of Man.

HOLY BIBLE-JM

16 And God the Eternal laid a command upon the man; "You are free to eat from any tree in the park," he said, 17 "but you must not eat from the tree that yields knowledge of good and evil, for on the day you eat from that tree you shall die." 18 Then said God the Eternal,   "It is not good for man to be alone; I will make a helper to suit him."

2:18
    And the Lord God said,"It is not good
that Adam should be alone. I will make for
v.1:20
him a separate group of **ANIMALS**, and also
I will make for him, his counterpart."

2:19
    And out of the ground, the Lord God
v.7
FORMED all the domesticated farm animals.
And He brought them to Adam to see what
he would call them: and whatsoever Adam
called them, that was their name.

2:20
    And Adam gave names to all the
domesticated animals God gave him,
but Adam still did not have a mate
for himself.

2:21
    So the Lord God caused a deep sleep
(curve,chunk)
to fall upon Adam, and God took a   **RIB**
out of his side, and then closed up his
flesh.

2:22
    And the Lord God **FORMED** a woman out
of the curve He took from Adam, then
brought the woman unto him.

2:23
    And Adam said,"This is now bones of
my bones; and flesh of my flesh: and I
will call her woman, because she was
taken out of man."

24 Therefore shall a man leave his father and his mother, and shall cleave unto his wife: and they shall be one flesh. 25 And they were both naked, the man and his wife, and were not ashamed. 3:1 Now the serpent was more subtil than any beast of the field which the Lord God had made. And he said unto the woman, Yea, hath God said, Ye shall not eat of every tree of the garden? 2 And the woman said unto the serpent, We may eat of the fruit of the trees of the garden: 3 But of the fruit of the tree which is in the midst of the garden, God hath said, Ye shall not eat of it, neither shall ye touch it, lest ye die.

24 Therefore a man leaves his father and his mother and cleaves to his wife, and they become one flesh. 25 And the man and his wife were both naked, and were not ashamed. 3:1 Now the serpent was more subtle than any other wild creature that the Lord God had made. He said to the woman, "Did God say, 'You shall not eat of any tree of the garden'?" 2 And the woman said to the serpent, "We may eat of the fruit of the trees of the garden; 3 but God said, 'You shall not eat of the fruit of the tree which is in the midst of the garden, neither shall you touch it, lest you die.'"

24 Hence a man leaves his father and mother and clings to his wife, so that they become one flesh. 25 The two of them were naked, the man and his wife, yet they felt no shame. 3:1 Now the serpent was the shrewdest of all the wild beasts that the Lord God had made. He said to the woman, "Did God really say: You shall not eat of any tree of the garden?" 2 The woman replied to the serpent, "We may eat of the fruit of the other trees of the garden. 3 It is only about fruit of the tree in the middle of the garden that God said: 'You shall not eat of it or touch it, lest you die,'"

24 Therefore shall a man leave his father and his mother, and shall cleave unto his wife, and they shall be one flesh. 25 And they were both naked, Adam and his wife, and were not ashamed. 3:1 Now the serpent was more subtle than all the wild beasts that the Lord God had made. And the serpent said to the woman, Truly has God said that you shall not eat of any tree of the garden? 2 And the woman said to the serpent, We may eat of the fruit of all the trees of the garden; 3 But of the fruit of the tree which is in the midst of the garden, God has said, You shall not eat of it, neither shall you touch it, lest you die.

19 So from the ground God shaped every wild beast and every bird of the air, bringing them to the man to see what he would call them; whatever the man called any living creature, that was to be its name. 20 So the man named all the animals and the birds and every wild beast, but no helper could be found to suit man himself. 21 Then God the Eternal made a deep sleep to fall upon the man; while he slept, He took one of his ribs, closing up the flesh in its place; 22 the rib He had taken from the man God the Eternal shaped into a woman, and brought her to the man. 23 Then said the man, This, this at last, is bone of my bones, and flesh of my own flesh: this shall be called Wo-man, for from man was she taken! 24 (This is why a man leaves his father and mother and cleaves to his wife, till they become one flesh.) 25 Both of them, the man and his wife, were naked, but they felt no shame. 3:1 Now the serpent was cunning, more cunning than any creature that God the Eternal had made; he said to the woman, "And so God has said that you are not to eat fruit from any tree in the park?" 2 The woman said to the serpent, "We can eat fruit from the trees in the park, 3 but, as for the tree in the centre of the park, God has said, 'You must not eat from it, you must not touch it, lest you die,'"

2:24
    Therefore shall a man leave his father
and his mother, and shall cleave unto his
wife: and they shall be one flesh.

2:25
    And they were both nude, the man and
his wife, and knowing only good; were
not ashamed before God.

CHAPTER THREE
3:1   (Satan)
    But the **SERPENT** was wiser than any
living being of the field which the Lord
God had made. And knowing evil, and not
ashamed to question the truth of God's
word, he said unto the woman. "Can it be
that God has said: you can not partake of
the **FRUIT** of every **TREE** in the garden?"

3:2
    And the woman said to Satan,"Of every
             [Adam present]
TREE of the garden, **WE** may freely
partake of,

3:3
    But of the **TREE** with the knowledge of
                                      5060
good and evil, we shall not **TOUCH** or
partake of his **FRUIT**, because in the day
we partake of it, we shall surely die."

1) 5060
   naga
   to lie with,
   to have sex.

(24)

4 And the serpent said unto the woman, Ye shall not surly die: 5 For God doth know that in the day ye eat thereof, then your eyes shall be opened, and ye shall be as gods, knowing good and evil. 6 And then the woman saw that the tree was good for food, and that it was pleasant to the eyes, and a tree to be desired to make one wise, she took of the fruit thereof, and did eat, and gave also unto her husband with her; and he did eat. 7 And the eyes of them both were opened, and they knew that they were naked; and they sewed fig leaves together, and made themselves aprons. 8 And they heard the voice of the Lord God walking in the garden in the cool of the day: and Adam and his wife hid themselves from the presence of the Lord God amongst the trees of the garden.

4 But the serpent said to the woman, "You will not die. 5 For God knows that when you eat of it your eyes will be opened, and you will be like God, knowing good and evil." 6 So when the woman saw that the tree was good for food, and that it was a delight to the eyes, and that the tree was to be desired to make one wise, she took of its fruit and ate; and she also gave some to her husband, and he ate. 7 Then the eyes of both were opened, and they knew that they were naked; and they sewed fig leaves together and made themselves aprons. 8 And they heard the sound of the Lord God walking in the garden in the cool of the day, and the man and his wife hid themselves from the presence of the Lord God among the trees of the garden.

4 And the serpent said to the woman, "You are not going to die, 5 but God knows that as soon as you eat of it your eyes will be opened and you will be like divine beings who know good and bad." 6 When the woman saw that the tree was good for eating and a delight to the eyes, and that the tree was desirable as a source of wisdom, she took of its fruit and ate. She also gave some to her husband, and he ate. 7 Then the eyes of both of them were opened and they perceived that they were naked; and they sewed together fig leaves and made themselves loincloths. 8 They heard the sound of the Lord God moving about in the garden at the breezy time of day; and the man and his wife hid from the Lord God among the trees of the garden.

4 And the serpent said to the woman, You shall not surly die; 5 For God knows that in the day you eat of it, your eyes shall be opened, and you shall be like gods, knowing good and evil. 6 So when the woman saw that the tree was good for food, and that it was pleasant to the eyes, and that the tree was delightful to look at, she took of the fruit thereof, and did eat, and she also gave to her husband with her; and he did eat. 7 Then the eyes of them both were opened, and they knew that they were naked; and they sewed fig leaves together, and made themselves aprons. 8 And they heard the voice of the Lord God walking in the garden in the cool of the day; and Adam and his wife hid themselves from the presence of the Lord God among the trees of the garden.

4 "No," said the serpent to the woman, "you shall not die; 5 God knows that on the day you eat from it your eyes will be opened and you will be like gods, knowing good and evil." 6 So, when the woman saw that the tree was good to eat and delightful to see, desirable to look upon, she took some of the fruit and ate it; she also gave some to her husband, and he ate. 7 Then the eyes of both were opened, and they realized that they were naked; so they stitched some fig leaves together and made themselves girdles. 8 In the cool of the day, when they heard the sound of God the Eternal walking in the park, the man and his wife hid from the presence of God the Eternal among the trees of the park;

3:4
   And Satan said to the woman,"You shall

not surely die.

3:5
   For God know's that in the day you

partake of it, then your eyes shall be

open.[open to wickedness, closed to truth]

And you will be as God, with the knowledge

of good and evil."

3:6
   And the woman's eyes and mind lusted

after Satan's seductive beauty and

knowledge. And Satan did seduce, and had

sexual relations with the woman, and she

convinced Adam to partake of also.

3:7   v.5
   And the eyes of them both were **OPENED:**
                      v.2:5
and they knew before that they were **NUDE,**

but because of the knowledge now received,

they felt **NAKED** and ashamed of what they

had done. So they both sewed together

Fig leaves and made aprons to cover

their genitals.

3:8
   And they heard the footsteps of the

Lord God walking in the garden, so they

hid themselves among the Fig trees.

9 And the Lord God called unto Adam, and said unto him, Where art thou? 10 And he said, I heard thy voice in the garden, and I was afraid, because I was naked; and I hid myself. 11 And He said, Who told thee that thou wast naked? Hast thou eaten of the tree, whereof I commanded thee that thou shouldest not eat? 12 And the man said, The woman whom thou gavest to be with me, she gave me of the tree, and I did eat. 13 And the Lord God said unto the woman, What is this that thou has done? And the woman said, The serpent be guild me, and I did eat. 14 And the Lord God said unto the serpent, Because thou hast done this, thou art cursed above all cattle, and every beast of the field; upon thy belly shalt thou go, and dust shalt thou eat all the days of thy life:

9 But the Lord God called to the man, and said to him, "Where are you?" 10 And he said, "I heard the sound of thee in the garden, and I was afraid, because I was naked; and I hid myself." 11 He said, "Who told you that you were naked? Have you eaten of the tree of which I commanded you not to eat?" 12 The man said, "The woman whom thou gavest to be with me, she gave me fruit of the tree, and I ate." 13 Then the Lord God said to the woman, What is this that you have done?" The woman said, "The serpent beguiled me, and I ate." 14 The Lord God said to the serpent, "Because you have done this, cursed are you above all cattle, and above all wild animals; upon your belly you shall go, and dust you shall eat all the days of your life.

9 The Lord God called out to the man and said to him, "Where are you?" 10 He replied, "I heard the sound of You in the garden, and I was afraid because I was naked, so I hid." 11 Then He asked, "Who told you that you were naked? Did you eat of the tree from which I had forbidden you to eat?" 12 The man said, "The woman You put at my side-she gave me of the tree, and I ate." 13 And the Lord God said to the woman, "What is this you have done!" The woman replied, "The serpent duped me, and I ate." 14 Then the Lord God said to the serpent, "Because you did this, more cursed shall you be than all cattle and all the wild beast: On your belly shall you crawl and dirt shall you eat all the days of your life.

9 And the Lord God called to Adam, and said to him, Where are you, Adam? 10 And he said, I heard thy voice in the garden, and when I saw that I was naked, I hid myself. 11 And the Lord God said to him, Who told you that you were naked? Have you eaten of the tree of which I commanded you that you should not eat? 12 And Adam said, The woman whom thou gavest to be with me, she gave me of the fruit of the tree, and I did eat. 13 And the Lord God said to the woman, What is this that you have done? And the woman said, The serpent beguiled me, and I did eat. 14 And the Lord God said to the serpent, Because you have done this thing, cursed are you above all cattle, and above all beast of the field; on your belly shall you go, and dust shall you eat all the days of your life;

9 but God the Eternal called to the man and asked him, "Where are you?" 10 "I heard thy sound within the park," he answered, "and I was afraid, because I was naked; so I hid myself." 11 He said, "Who told you that you were naked? Have you been eating from the tree which I forbade you to eat?" 12 The man said, "The woman thou gavest me as a companion, she gave me some fruit from the tree, and I ate it." 13 Then God the Eternal said to the woman, "What is this that you have done?" The woman said, "I ate because the serpent beguiled me." 14 So God the Eternal said to the serpent, "Since you have done this, A curse on you of all creatures! a curse on you of all beasts! On your belly shall you crawl and eat dust all your days!

3:9
  And the Lord God; knowing where they were, called out,"Adam, where are you?"

3:10
  And Adam said,"I heard you coming and we hid ourselves because we were afraid and we were naked."

3:11
  And the Lord God said,"Who told you that you were naked? Have you partaken of the **TREE** with the knowledge of good and evil?"

3:12
  And Adam said,"I was persuaded by the woman you gave to me, and I did partake of with her."

3:13
  And the Lord God said unto the woman, "What is this you have done?" And the woman said,"The **SERPENT** (Satan) **BEGUILED** 5377 me and I did partake.

3:14
  And without asking any questions, the Lord God said unto Satan,"Because you have done this evil thing, you are cursed as the lowest and most disgusting form of life which I have made.

NOTE:
BEGUILED
II Cor. 11:3
But I fear,
lest by any
means, as the
(Satan) 1818
SERPENT BEGUILED
Eve through his
subtilty, so your
minds should be
corrupted from
the simplicity
that is in Christ.

1) 5377
  nasha
  to seduce
  sexually.

2) 1818 (GR)
  exapatao
  to seduce,
  to have sex
  with.

15 And I will put enmity between thee and the woman, and between thy seed and her seed; it shall bruise thy head, and thou shall bruise his heel. 16 Unto the woman he said, I will greatly multiply thy sorrow and thy conception; in sorrow thou shalt bring forth children; and thy desire shall be to thy husband, and he shall rule over thee. 17 And unto Adam he said, Because thou hast hearkened unto the voice of thy wife, and hast eaten of the tree, of which I commanded thee, saying, Thou shalt not eat of it: cursed is the ground for thy sake; in sorrow shalt thou eat of it all the days of thy life; 18 Thorns also and thistles shall it bring forth to thee; and thou shalt eat the herb of the field;

15 I will put enmity between you and the woman, and between your seed and her seed; he shall bruise your head, and you shall bruise his heel." 16 To the woman he said, "I will greatly multiply your pain in childbearing; in pain you shall bring forth children, yet your desire shall be for your husband, and he shall rule over you." 17 And to Adam he said, "Because you have listened to the voice of your wife, and have eaten of the tree of which I commanded you, shall not eat of it,' cursed is the ground because of you; in toil you shall eat of it all the days of your life; 18 Thorns and thistles it shall bring forth to you; and you shall eat the plants of the field.

15 I will put enmity between you and the woman, And between your offspring and hers; They shall strike at your head, And you shall strike at their heel." 16 And to the woman He said, "I will make most severe your pangs in childbearing; In pain shall you bear children. Yet your urge shall be for your husband, And he shall rule over you." 17 To Adam He said, "Because you did as your wife said and ate of the tree about which I commanded you, 'You shall not eat of it, 'Cursed be the ground because of you; By toil shall you eat of it all the days of your life: 18 Thorns and thistles shall it sprout for you. But your food shall be the grasses of the field;

15 And I will put enmity between your posterity and her posterity; her posterity shall tread your head under foot, and you shall strike him in his heel. 16 To the woman he said, I will greatly multiply your pain and your conception; in pain you shall bring forth children, and you shall be dependent on your husband, and he shall rule over you. 17 And to Adam he said, Because you have listened to the voice of your wife, and have eaten of the tree of which I commanded you, saying, You shall not eat of it, cursed is the ground for your sake; in sorrow shall you eat the fruits of it all the days of your life; 18 Thorns also and thistles shall it bring forth to you; and you shall eat the herbs of the field;

15 And I will set a feud between you and the woman, between your brood and hers: they shall strike at your head, and you shall strike at their heel." 16 To the woman he said, "I will make child-birth a sore pain for you, you shall have pangs in bearing; yet you shall crave to your husband, and he shall master you." 17 To the man he said, "Since you have listened to what your wife said, eating from the tree of which I forbade you to eat, Cursed is the ground on your account, you shall suffer all your life, as you win food from it; 18 thorns and thistles shall it bear for you, and you must eat plants of the field;
19 in the sweat of your brow you shall earn you food, till you return to the ground from which you were taken; for dust you are, and you return to dust." 20 [[The man called the name of his wife Eve (Life), because she was the mother of all living persons.]] 21 [[And God the Eternal made skin tunics for the man and his wife, and clothed them.]]

3:15

And I will put enmity between you and the woman, and between **YOUR CHILDREN** and **HER CHILDREN**. And out of the woman's seed shall come **THE CHRIST**, (Yahshua) and He shall completely destroy you and all your evil works."

3:16

"Unto the woman, I will greatly multiply the pain in pregnancy. And in pain shall you bring forth children, and your desire shall be subject to your husband, and he shall rule over you."

3:17

"And unto you Adam, because you have hearken unto the voice of your wife, and have partaken of with her, cursed is **THE GROUND** you till. In sorrow shall you eat of it all the days of your life."

3:18

"Thorns and poisonous weeds and insects will you have to deal with, and you shall eat the herbs and vegetation of the **FIELDS** and not the **FRUITS** of the **GARDEN PARADISE.**

NOTE:
Matt. 13:37-40
John 8:44
I John 3:1-24

COMMENT:
If it was only an apple Adam and Eve partook of, why would Yahveh greatly multiply the pain in child birth?

30

19 In the sweat of thy face shalt thou eat bread, till thou return unto the ground; for out of it wast thou taken: for dust thou art, and unto dust shalt thou return. 20 And Adam called his wife's name Eve; because she was the mother of all living. 21 Unto Adam also and to his wife did the Lord God make coats of skins, and clothed them.22 And the Lord God said, Behold, the man is become as one of us, to know good and evil: and now, lest he put forth his hand, and take also of the tree of life, and eat, and live for ever: 23 Therefore the Lord God sent him forth from the garden of Eden, to till the ground from whence he was taken.

19 In the sweat of your face you shall eat bread till you return to the ground, for out of it you were taken; you are dust, and to dust you shall return." 20 The man called his wife's name Eve, because she was the mother of all living. 21 And the Lord God made for Adam and for his wife garments of skins, and clothed them. 22 Then the Lord God said, "Behold, the man has become like one of us, knowing good and evil; and now, lest he put forth his hand and take also of the tree of life, and eat, and live for ever— 23 therefore the Lord God sent him forth from the garden of Eden, to till the ground from which he was taken.

19 By the sweat of your brow shall you get bread to eat, until you return to the groundfor from it you were taken. For dust you are, and to dust you shall return," 20 The man named his wife Eve, because she was the mother of all the living. 21 And the Lord God made garments of skins for Adam and his wife, and clothed them. 22 And the Lord God said, "Now that the man has become like one of us, knowing good and bad, what if he should stretch out his hand and take also from the tree of life and eat, and live forever!" 23 So the Lord God banished him from the garden of Eden, to till the soil from which he was taken.

19 In the sweat of your face shall you eat bread, until you return to the ground; out of it you were taken; for dust you are, and to dust shall you return. 20 So Adam called his wife's name Eve because she was the mother of all living. 21 And the Lord God made for Adam and for his wife coats of skins, and clothed them. 22 Then the Lord God said, Behold, the man has become like one of us, to know good and evil; and now, lest he put forth his hand, and take also of the tree of life, and eat, and live forever; 23 Therefore the Lord God sent him forth from the garden of Eden, to till the ground from whence he was taken.

22 Then said God the Eternal, "Man has become like one of us, he knows good and evil. He might reach his hand now to the tree of life also, and by eating of it live for ever!" 23 So God the Eternal expelled him from the park of Eden, to till the ground from which he had been taken; 24 he drove the man out, and set kherubs at the east of the park of Eden, with the blade of a sword flashing in every direction, to guard the path to the tree of life. 4:1 Now the man had intercourse with his wife Eve; she conceived and bore Cain (GOT), saying, "I have got a man from the Eternal." 2 Next she bore his brother Abel. Abel was a shepherd, while Cain was a farmer. 3 In course of time, Cain brought some produce of the ground as a present to the Eternal, 4 while Abel brought some of the firstborn from his flock, that is , some fat slices from them. The Eternal favoured Abel and his present; 5 he did not favour Cain and his. So Cain was furious and downcast. 6 "Why are you furious? said the Eternal to Cain, "why are you downcast? 7 If your heart is honest, you would surly look bright? If you are sullen, sin is lying in wait for you, eager to be at you—yet you ought to master it." 8 But Cain quarreled with his brother Abel, and when they were out in the open country, Cain attacked his brother Abel and killed him.

3:19
    With hard work and sweat will you
have to endure to feed yourself until
you die and return unto the ground from
where you came. For dust you are and to
dust you shall return."

3:20
    And Adam called his wife's name Eve;
which means **LIFE**, because threw her seed
would some day in the future bring forth
Yahshua: the only one who could redeem a
man, dead in sin and give him back **LIFE**
threw repentance.

3:21
    And the Lord God made Adam and his
wife Eve, coats of skin, and clothed them
both.

3:22
    And the Lord God said,"Behold, Adam
has become as one of us; to know good and
evil, and if he partakes now of the
(Yahshua)
TREE OF LIFE he will live forever in his
fallen state."

3:23
    Therefore the Lord God drove Adam and
his wife Eve, out of the **GARDEN PARADISE**

NOTE:
This is the first
BLOOD SACRIFICE for
the forgiveness of
sin, as was done in
the Old Testament.

YAHSHUA IS OUR
BLOOD SACRIFICE
OF TODAY.

32

24 So he drove out the man; and he placed at the east of the garden of Eden Cherubims, and a flaming sword which turned every way, to keep the way of the tree of life. 4:1 And Adam knew Eve his wife; and she conceived, and bare Cain, and said, I have gotten a man from the Lord. 2 And she again bare his brother Abel. And Abel was a keeper of sheep, but Cain was a tiller of the ground. 3 And in process of time it came to pass, that Cain brought of the fruit of the ground an offering unto the Lord. 4 And Abel, he also brought of the firstlings of his flock and of the fat thereof. And the Lord had respect unto Abel and to his offering:

24 He drove out the man; and at the east of the garden of Eden he placed the cherubim, and a flaming sword which turned every way, to guard the way to the tree of life. 4:1 Now Adam knew Eve his wife, and she conceived and bore Cain, saying, "I have gotten a man with the help of the Lord." 2 And again, she bore his brother Abel. Now Abel was a keeper of sheep, and Cain a tiller of the ground. 3 In the course of time Cain brought to the Lord an offering of the fruit of the ground, 4 and Abel brought of the firstlings of his flock and of their fat portions. And the Lord had regard for Abel and his offering,

24 He drove the man out, and stationed east of the garden of Eden the cherubim and the fiery ever-turning sword, to guard the way to the tree of life. 4:1 Now the man knew his wife Eve, and she conceived and bore Cain, saying, "I have gained a male child with the help of the Lord." 2 She then bore his brother Abel. Abel became a keeper of sheep, and Cain became a tiller of the soil. 3 In the course of time, Cain brought an offering to the Lord from the fruit of the soil; 4 and Abel, for his part, brought the choicest of the firstlings of his flock. The Lord paid heed to Abel and his offering,

24 So the Lord God drove out the man; and he placed at the east of the garden of Eden Cherubim, and a flaming sword which turned every way, to guard the path to the tree of life. 4:1 And Adam knew Eve his wife; and she conceived, and bore Cain, and said, I have gotten a man for the Lord. 2 And she again bore his brother Abel. And Abel was a keeper of sheep, but Cain was a tiller of the ground. 3 And in the course of time it came to pass that Cain brought of the fruit of the ground an offering to the Lord. 4 And Abel also brought of the firstborn of his flock and of the fatlings thereof. And the Lord was pleased with Abel and with his offering;

9 Then the Eternal asked Cain, "Where is your brother Abel?" "How do I know?" said Cain; "am I a shepherd to my brother?" 10 He answered, "What have you done? Listen, your brother's blood is crying to Me from the soil! 11 And now you are cursed off the country that has opened to swallow down the brother's blood you shed; 12 after this, the fields will not yield you their produce, when you till them; you must go stumbling and straying over the earth."

3:24   (Yahveh)
    And the **LORD GOD** placed in the
    [type of angel]
garden, a   **CHERUBIM**   with a flaming sword

which turned every way to preserve and
                              (Yahshua)
protect the path to the **TREE OF LIFE**.

CHAPTER FOUR
4:1
    And because of Eve's sexual relations

with Satan, she conceived and gave birth

to **CAIN**, and said,"I have gotten a man

with the help of the Lord."

4:2
    Then she continued in giving birth

to Cain's   **FRATERNAL** twin brother, Abel,

who became a keeper of sheep, while Cain

became a tiller of the ground.

4:3
    And at appointed times, it came to

pass that Cain; in his own way, would

bring from his fields, a love offering

to the Lord, but the offerings were not

the best of his field.

4:4
    And Abel, at this same time, also

brought love offerings. And his

offerings were the first born and the

healthiest of his flocks. So the Lord

had respect for Abel's love offerings

and accepted them by fire.

NOTE:
FRATERNAL TWINS
Twins which are
conceived by a
woman, but
impregnated by
two separate
males.

5 But of Cain and to his offering he had not respect. And Cain was very wroth, and his countenance fell. 6 And the Lord said unto Cain, Why art thou wroth? and why is thy countenance fallen? 7 If thou doest well, shalt thou not be accepted? and if thou doest not well, sin lieth at the door. And unto thee shall be his desire, and thou shalt rule over him. 8 And Cain talked to Abel his brother: and it came to pass, when they were in the field, that Cain rose up against Abel his brother, and slew him. 9 And the Lord said unto Cain, Where is Abel thy brother? And he said, I know not: Am I my brother's keeper? 10 And he said, What hast thou done? the voice of thy brother's blood crieth unto me from the ground.

5 but for Cain and his offering he had no regard. So Cain was very angry, and his countenance fell. 6 The Lord said to Cain, "Why are you angry, and why has your countenance fallen? 7 If you do well, will you not be accepted? And if you do not well, sin is couching at the door; its desire is for you, but you must master it." 8 Cain said to Abel his brother, "Let us go out to the field." And when they were in the field, Cain rose up against his brother Abel, and killed him. 9 Then the Lord said to Cain, "Where is Abel your brother?" He said, "I do not know; am I my brother's keeper?" 10 And the Lord said, "What have you done? The voice of your brother's blood is crying to me from the ground."

5 but to Cain and his offering He paid no heed. Cain was much distressed and his face fell. 6 And the Lord said to Cain, "Why are you distressed, And why is your face fallen? 7 Surely, if you do right, there is uplift. But if you do not do right, sin couches at the door; Its urge is toward you, Yet you can be its master." 8 Cain said to his brother Abel... and when they were in the field, Cain set upon his brother Abel and killed him. 9 The Lord said to Cain, "Where is your brother Abel?" And he said, "I do not know. Am I my brother's keeper?" 10 Then He said, "What have you done? Hark, your brother's blood cries out to Me from the ground!

5 But with Cain and with his offering he was not pleased. So Cain was exceedingly displeased, and his countenance was sad. 6 And the Lord said to Cain, Why are you displeased? and why is your countenance sad? 7 Behold, if you do well, shall you not be accepted? and if you do not well, sin lies at the door. You should return to your brother, and he shall be subject to you. 8 And Cain said to Abel his brother, Let us go to the plain; and it came to pass, when they were in the field, that Cain rose up against Abel his brother, and slew him. 9 And the Lord said to Cain, Where is Abel your brother? And he said, I do not know. Am I my brother's keeper? 10 And the Lord said, What have you done? The voice of your brother's blood cries to me from the ground.

4:5
    But Cain's offerings were not accepted

and would not burn. And this made Cain

very angry, and his countenance fell.

4:6
    And the Lord asked Cain,"Why are you

angry? And why has your countenance fallen?

4:7
    If you are honest your offering will be

accepted. But if you are dishonest sin is

at your door." [Honesty, devotion, and

your love is what Yahveh desires of you.]

4:8
    And Cain being angry, said unto his

brother Abel,"Let's go out into the field."

And it came to pass when they were out

there, Cain rose up against Abel and
      v.9:6
MURDERED him.

4:9
    And Yahveh; knowing what had happened

and having Abel now with Him, said unto

Cain, "Where is Abel your brother?" And

Cain lying to Yahveh said,"I know not:

am I my brother's keeper?"

4:10
    And Yahveh said to Cain,"What have

you done? Your brother's righteous blood

cries unto Me from the ground.

11 And now art thou cursed from the earth, which hath opened her mouth to receive thy brother's blood from thy hand; 12 When thou tillest the ground, it shall not henceforth yield unto thee her strength; a fugitive and a vagabond shalt thou be in the earth. 13 and Cain said unto the Lord, My punishment is greater than I can bear. 14 Behold, thou hast driven me out this day from the face of the earth; and from thy face shall I be hid; and I shall be a fugitive and a vagabond in the earth; and it shall come to pass, that every one that findeth me shall slay me. 15 And the Lord said unto him, Therefore whosoever slayeth Cain, vengeance shall be taken on him sevenfold. And the Lord set a mark upon Cain, lest any finding him should kill him. 16 And Cain went out from the presence of the Lord, and dwelt in the land of Nod, on the east of Eden.

11 And now you are cursed from the ground, which has opened its mouth to receive your brother's blood from your hand. 12 When you till the ground, it shall no longer yield to you its strength; you shall be a fugitive and a wanderer on the earth." 13 Cain said to the Lord, "My punishment is greater than I can bear. 14 Behold, thou hast driven me this day away from the ground; and from thy face I shall be hidden; an I shall be fugitive and a wanderer on the earth, and whoever finds me will slay me." 15 Then the Lord said to him, 'Not so! If any one slays Cain, vengeance shall be taken on him sevenfold." And the Lord put a mark on Cain, lest any who came upon him should kill him. 16 Then Cain went away from the presence of the Lord, and dwelt in the land of Nod, east of Eden.

11 Therefore, you shall be more cursed than the ground, which opened its mouth to received your brother's blood from your hand. 12 If you till the soil, it shall no longer yield its strength to you. You shall become a ceaseless wanderer on earth." 13 Cain said to the Lord, "My punishment is to great to bear! 14 Since You have banished me this day from the soil, and I must avoid Your presence and become a restless wanderer on earth —anyone who meets me may kill me!" 15 The Lord said to him, "I promise, if anyone kills Cain, sevenfold vengeance shall be taken on him." And the Lord put a mark on Cain, lest anyone who met him should kill him. 16 Cain left the presence of the Lord and settled in the land of Nod, east of Eden. **HOLY BIBLE-GML**

11 And from henceforth, you are cursed from the earth, which has opened its mouth to receive your brother's blood from your hand; 12 When you till the ground, it shall no more yield to you its strength; a fugitive and a wanderer shall you be on the earth. 13 And Cain said to the Lord, My transgression is to great to be forgiven. 14 Behold, thou hast driven me out this day from the face of the land; and from thy face shall I be hidden; and I shall be a fugitive and a wanderer on the earth; and it shall come to pass, that whoever finds me shall slay me. 15 And the Lord said to him, It shall not be so; whoever slays Cain, vengeance shall be taken on him sevenfold. And the Lord set a mark upon Cain, so that anyone who may find him may not kill him. 16 And Cain went out from the presence of the Lord, and dwelt in the land of Nod, on the east of Eden. **HOLY BIBLE-JM**

11 And now you are cursed off the country that has opened to swallow down the brother's blood you shed; 12 after this, the fields will not yield you their produce, when you till them; you must go stumbling and straying over the earth." 13 Cain said to the Eternal, "My punishment is more than I can bear. 14 Thou art expelled me from thy sight; I must go stumbling and straying over the earth, and anyone who catches me will kill me." 15 So the Eternal said to him, "Well then, whoever kills Cain, seven times over shall the murder be avenged"; and the Eternal set a mark on Cain, to prevent anyone from catching and killing him. 16 Then Cain left the presence of the Eternal to stay in Nod (Wanderland), east of Eden.

4:11
    And now, because you have done this

evil thing, you shall be cursed more
       v.3:17
than the **GROUND;** which has opened her

mouth to receive your brother's blood.

4:12
    When you cultivate the ground it

shall no longer yield unto you her

full strength: a fugitive and a wanderer

shall you be."

4:13
    And Cain said unto the Lord,"Is my

iniquity too great to be forgiven?

4:14
    Behold, this day the Lord has driven

me out of my homeland, and from God's

face shall I hide. I shall be a fugitive

and a wanderer, and it shall come to pass

that everyone I meet will want to slay me."

4:15
    And the Lord said unto Cain,"Not so,

for whosoever slays Cain, vengeance shall

be taken out on him sevenfold." And Yahveh

put a mark upon Cain so that anyone

finding him should not kill him.

4:16
    And Cain went out from the presence

of the Lord and dwelt in the land of the

Nomads, east of Eden.

17 And Cain knew his wife; and she conceived, and bare Enoch: and he builded a city, and called the name of the city, after the name of his son, Enoch. 18 And unto Enoch was born Irad: and Irad begat Mehujael: and Mehujael begat Methusael: and Methusael begat Lamech. 19 And Lamech took unto him two wives: the name of the one was Adah, and the name of the other Zillah. 20 And Adah bare Jabal: he was the father of such as dwell in tents, and of such as have cattle. 21 And his brother's name was Jubal: he was the father of all such as handle the harp and organ. 22 And Zillah, she also bare Tubal-cain, an instructor of every artificer in brass and iron: and the sister of Tubal-cain was Naamah. 23 And Lamech said unto his wives, Adah and Zillah, Hear my voice; ye wives of Lamech, hearken unto my speech: for I have slain a man to my wounding, and a young man to my hurt.

RSV

17 Cain knew his wife, and she conceived and bore Enoch; and he built a city, and called the name of the city after the name of his son, Enoch. 18 To Enoch was born Irad; and Irad was the father of Mehujael, and Mehujael the father of Methushael, and Methushael the father of Lamech. 19 And Lamech took two wives; the name of the one was Adah, and the name of the other Zillah. 20 Adah bore Jabel; he was the father of those who dwell in tents and have cattle. 21 His brother's name was Jubal; he was the father of all those who play the lyre and pipe. 22 Zillah bore Tubal-cain; he was the forger of all instruments of bronze and iron. The sister of Tubal-cain was Naamah. 23 Lamech said to his wives: "Adah and Zillah, hear my voice; you wives of Lamech, hearken to what I say: I have slain a man for wounding me, a young man for striking me.

TANAKH

17 Cain knew his wife, and she conceived and bore Enoch. And he then founded a city, and named the city after his son Enoch. 18 To Enoch was born Irad, and Irad begot Mehujael, and Mehujael begot Methusael, and Methusael begot Lamech. 19 Lamech took to himself two wives: the name of the one was Adah, and the name of the other was Zillah. 20 Adah bore Jabal; he was the ancestor of those who dwell in tents and amidst herds. 21 And the name of his brother was Jubal; he was the ancestor of all who played the lyre and the pipe. 22 As for Zillah, she bore Tubal-cain, who forged all implements of copper and iron. And the sister of Tubal-cain was Naamah. 23 And Lamech said to his wives, "Adah and Zillah, hear my voice; O wives of Lamech, give ear to my speech. I have slain a man for wounding me, And a lad for bruising me.

HOLY BIBLE-GML

17 And Cain knew his wife; and she conceived, and bore Enoch; and he started to build a village, and named the village after the name of his son, Enoch. 18 And to Enoch was born Irad; and Irad begot Mehujael; and Mehujael begot Methusael: and Methusael begot Lamech. 19 And Lamech took two wives: the name of the one was Adah, and the name of the other Zillah. 20 And Adah bore Jabal, who was the father of those who dwell in tents, and are owners of cattle. 21 And his brother's name was Jubal; he was the father of all those who play the guitar and harp. 22 And Zillah also bore Tubal-cain was Naamah. 23 And Lamech said to his wives, Adah and Zillah, Hear my voice; you wives of Lamech, hearken to my speech; for I have killed a man by wounding him, and a boy by beating him.

HOLY BIBLE-JM

17 When Cain had intercourse with his wife, she conceived and bore Hanok; Cain built a town and called it after his son Hanok. 18 Irad was born to Hanok, and Irad was the father of Mehujael, Mehujael the father of Methushael, and Methushael the father of Lemek. 19 Lemek married two wives; the name of one was Adah, the name of the other Zillah. 20 (Adah bore Jabal, the ancestor of shepherds who live in tents: 21 his brother's name was Jubal, the ancestor of all who play the lyre and the pipe.

4:17
And Cain took a wife. A woman from
v.1:26
one of the **SIXTH DAY RACES**, and she gave

birth to Enoch: and Cain also built and

named the first city after him.

4:18
And unto Enoch was born Irad: and Irad

begat Mehujael, and Mehujael, begat

Methusael, and Methusael begat Lamech.

4:19
And Lamech; the first polygamist, took

to wife Adah and Zillah.

4:20
And Adah bare Jabal, who was the father

of such that dwelt in tents and had cattle.

4:21
And his brother's name was Jubal; he

was the father of all that played musical

instruments.

4:22
And Zillah, she gave birth to

Tubal-Cain; which means, production of

Cain. He was a forger and craftsman in

brass and iron; and Naamah was the name

of his sister.

4:23
And Lamech said unto his wives; Adah

and Zillah,"Hearken unto **MY** voice, for I

have killed two men, and I am very proud

of it. One was killed for wounding me, and

the other for striking me.

24 If Cain shall be avenged sevenfold, truly Lamech seventy and seven fold.
25 And Adam knew his wife again; and she bare a son, and called his name Seth:
For God, said she, hath appointed me another seed instead of Abel, whom Cain
slew. 26 And to Seth, to him also there was born a son; and he called his name
Enos: then began men to call upon the name of the Lord. 5:1 This is the book
of the generations of Adam. In the day that God created man, in the likeness
of God made he him; 2 Male and female created he them; and blessed them, and
called their name Adam, in the day when they were created. 3 And Adam lived
130 years, and begat a son in his own likeness, after his image; and called
his name Seth: 4 And the days of Adam after he had begotten Seth were 800 years:
and he begat sons and daughters: 5 And all the days that Adam lived were 930
years: and he died. **RSV**

24 If Cain is avenged sevenfold, truly Lamech seventy-sevenfold. 25 And Adam
knew his wife again, and she bore a son and called his name Seth, for she said,
"God has appointed for me another child instead of Abel, for Cain slew him."
26 To Seth also a son was born, and he called his name Enosh. At that time men
began to call upon the name of the Lord. 5:1 This is the book of the generations
of Adam. When God created man, he made him in the likeness of God. 2 Male and
female he created them, and he blessed them and named them Man when they were
created. 3 When Adam had lived 130 years, he became the father of a son in his
own likeness, after his image, and named him Seth. 4 The days of Adam after
he became the father of Seth were 800 years; and he had other sons and daughters.
5 Thus all the days that Adam lived were 930 years; and he died.

24 If Cain is avenged sevenfold, then Lamech seventy-sevenfold. 25 Adam knew
his wife again, and she bore a son and named him Seth, meaning, "God has provided
me with another offspring in place of Abel," for Cain had killed him. 26 And
to Seth, in turn, a son was born, and he named him Enosh. It was then that men
began to invoke the Lord by name. 5:1 This is the record of Adam's line.— When
God created man, He made him in the likeness of God; 2 male and female He created
them. And when they were created, He blessed them and called them Man. 3 When
Adam had lived 130 years, he begot a son in his own likeness after his image,
and he named him Seth. 4 After the birth of Seth, Adam lived 800 years and begot
sons and daughters. 5 All the days that Adam lived came to 930 years; then he
died. **HOLY BIBLE-GML**

24 For if Cain is to be avenged sevenfold, then I Lamech seventy and sevenfold.
25 And Adam knew his wife Eve again; and she conceived and bore a son, and called
his name Seth; For God, she said, has given me another offspring instead of
Abel, whom Cain slew.26 And to Seth also there was born a son; and he called
his name Enosh. Then men began to call upon the name of the Lord. 5:1 This is
the book of the generations of Adam. In the day that God created man, in the
likeness of God created he him; 2 Male and female he created them; and God
blessed them, and called their name Adam, in the day when they were created.
3 And Adam lived 103 years, and begot a son in his own likeness, after his image;
and called his name Seth; 4 And Adam lived after he had begotten Seth 800 years;
and he begot sons and daughters. 5 Thus all the days that Adam lived were 930
years, and he died. **HOLY BIBLE-JM**

24 if Cain be avenged seven times, then seventy and seven times Lemek!"
25 Adam again had intercourse with his wife, who bore a son and called him Seth,
saying, "God has set up another child for me instead of Abel, whom Cain killed."
26 Seth also had a son born to him, called Enosh; he was the first to worship
the Eternal by name. 5:1 Here is the list of Adam's descendants. When God formed
man, he made him to resemble God; male and female, he formed them both and
blessed them, calling them human on the day when they were formed.

4:24
    And so if Cain shall be avenged

sevenfold, then I Lamech shall be avenged

seventy and seven fold."

NOTE:
This is the Genealogy of Cain, who was the offspring of Lucifer/ Satan. Better known as Kenites = SONS of CAIN.

CHAPTER FIVE
5:1
    This is the Genealogy of Adam, who was
v.2:7
FORMED in the **IMAGE** of God and in His
    (unfallen state = sinless)
          LIKENESS.

5:2
    And Adam was 130 years old when he
                              (fallen state)
begat a son in his own   **LIKENESS.**

And they called his name Seth, which

means; Compensation. "For God," Eve said,

"has appointed me another son to replace

Abel; whom Cain murdered."

5:3
    And Adam lived 800 years after the

birth of Seth. He fathered other sons

and daughters, and died at the age of 930.

5:4
    Seth at the age of 105 became the father

of Enos, which means; Frail/Incurable.

5:5
    At this time; men, including Enos, began

to profanely call upon the name of the Lord.

And loved their **MAN MADE GODS** more than the

true God; **YAHVEH.**

6 And Seth lived 105 years, and begat Enos: 7 And Seth lived after he begat Enos 807 years, and begat sons and daughters: 8 and all the days of Seth were 912 years: and he died. 9 And Enos lived 90 years, and begat Cainan: 10 And Enos lived after he begat Cainan 815 years, and begat sons and daughters: 11 And all the days of Enos were 905 years: and he died. 12 And Cainan lived 70 years, and begat Mahalaleel:

6 When Seth had lived 105 years, he became the father of Enosh. 7 Seth lived after the birth of Enosh 807 years, and had other sons and daughters. 8 Thus all the days of Seth were 912 years; and he died. 9 When Enosh had lived 90 years, he became the father of Kenan. 10 Enosh lived after the birth of Kenan 815 years, and had other sons and daughters. 11 Thus all the days of Enosh were 905 years; and he died. 12 When Kenan had lived 70 years, he became the father of Mahalalel.

6 When Seth had lived 105 years, he begot Enosh. 7 After the birth of Enosh, Seth lived 807 years and begot sons and daughters. 8 All the days of Seth came to 912 years; then he died. 9 When Enosh had lived 90 years, he begot Kenan. 10 After the birth of Kenan, Enosh lived 815 years and begot sons and daughters. 11 All the days of Enosh came to 905 years; then he died. 12 When Kenan had lived 70 years, he begot Mahalalel.

6 And Seth lived 105 years, and begot Enosh; 7 And Seth lived after he begot Enosh 807 years, and begot sons and daughters; 8 And all the days of Seth were 912 years, and he died. 9 And Enosh lived 90 years, and begot Cainan; 10 And Enosh lived after he begot Cainan 815 years, and begot sons and daughters; 11 And all the days of Enosh were 905 years, and he died. 12 And Cainan lived 70 years, and begot Mahlalael;

3 After living 130 years Adam became the father of a son resembling himself, in his own likeness, whom he called Seth; 4 Adam lived 800 years after the birth of Seth, and was the father of sons and daughters. 5 Thus Adam lived for 930 years in all; then he died. 6 After living 105 years Seth became the father of Enosh; 7 Seth lived 807 years after the birth of Enosh, and was the father of sons and daughters. 8 Thus Seth lived for 912 years in all; then he died.
9 After living 90 years Enosh became the father of Kenan; 10 Enosh lived 815 years after the birth of Kenan, and was the father of sons and daughters. 11 Thus Enosh lived for 905 years in all; then he died. 12 After living 70 years Kenan became the father of Mahalalel; 13 Kenan lived 840 years after the birth of Mahalalel, and was the father of sons and daughters. 14 Thus Kenan lived for 910 years in all; then he died. 15 After living 65 years Mahalalel became the father of Jared; 16 Mahalalel lived 830 years after the birth of Jared, and was the father of sons and daughters. 17 Thus Mahalalel lived for 895 years in all; then he died. 18 After living 162 years Jared became the father of Hanok;

5:6
　　Seth lived 807 years after the birth of Enos. He fathered other sons and daughters and died at the age of 912.

5:7
　　And Enos was 90 years old when he begat Cainan, which means; Possession or acquisition.

5:8
　　And Enos lived 815 years after the birth of Cainan. He fathered other sons and daughters and died at the age of 905.

5:9
　　And Cainan was 70 years old when he begat Mahalaleel, which means; Praise of God or God is splendor.

5:10
　　And Cainan lived 840 years after the birth of Mahalaleel. He fathered other sons and daughters and died at the age of 910.

5:11
　　And Mahalaleel was 65 years old when he begat Jared, which means; Descending or He that descends.

5:12
　　And Mahalaleel lived 830 years after the birth of Jared. He fathered other sons and daughters and died at the age of 895.

13 And Cainan lived after he begat Mahalaleel 840 years, and begat sons and daughters: 14 And all the days of Cainan were 910 years, and he died. 15 And Mahalaleel lived 65 years, and begat Jared: 16 And Mahalaleel lived after he begat Jared 830 years, and begat sons and daughters: 17 And all the days of Mahalaleel were 895 years, and he died. 18 And Jared lived 162 years, and he begat Enoch: 19 and Jared lived after he begat Enoch 800 years, and begat sons and daughters: 20 and all the days of Jared were 962 years: and he died. 21 And Enoch lived 65 years, and begat Methuselah: 22 and Enoch walked with God after he begat Methuselah 300 years, and begat sons and daughters: 23 and all the days of Enoch were 365 years: 24 and Enoch walked with God: and he was not; for God took him. 25 And Methuselah lived 187 years, and begat Lamech: 26 and Methuselah lived after he begat Lamech 782 years, and begat sons and daughters: 27 and all the days of Methuselah were 969 years: and he died.

13 Kenan lived after the birth of Mahalalel 840 years, and had other sons and daughters. 14 Thus all the days of Kenan were 910 years; and he died. 15 When Mahalalel had lived 65 years, he became the father of Jared. 16 Mahalalel lived after the birth of Jared 830 years, and had other sons and daughters. 17 Thus all the days of Mahalalel were 895 years; and he died. 18 When Jared had lived a 162 years, he became the father of Enoch. 19 Jared lived after the birth of Enoch 800 years, and had other sons and daughters. 20 Thus all the days of Jared were 962 years; and he died. 21 When Enoch had lived 65 years, he became the father of Methuselah. 22 Enoch walked with God after the birth of Methuselah 300 years, and had other sons and daughters. 23 Thus all the days of Enoch were 365 years. 24 Enoch walked with God ; and he was not, for God took him. 25 When Methuselah had lived 187 years, he became the father of Lamech. 26 Methuselah lived after the birth of Lamech 782 years, and had other sons and daughters. 27 Thus all the days of Methuselah were 969 years; and he died.

13 After the birth of Mahalalel, Kenan lived 840 years and begot sons and daughters. 14 All the days of Kenan came to 910 years; then he died. 15 When Mahalalel had lived 65 years, he begot Jared. 16 After the birth of Jared, Mahalalel lived 830 years and begot sons and daughters. 17 All the days of Mahalalel came to 895 years; then he died. 18 When Jared had lived 162 years, he begot Enoch. 19 After the birth of Enoch, Jared lived 800 years and begot sons and daughters. 20 All the days of Jared came to 962 years; then he died. 21 When Enoch had lived 65 years, he begot Methuselah. 22 After the birth of Methuselah, Enoch walked with God 300 years; and he begot sons and daughters. 23 All the days of Enoch came to 365 years. 24 Enoch walked with God; then he was no more, for God took him. 25 When Methuselah had lived 187 years, he begot Lamech. 26 After the birth of Lamech, Methuselah lived 782 years and begot sons and daughters. 27 All the days of Methuselah came to 969 years; then he died.

13 And Cainan lived after he begot Mahalalel 840 years, and begot sons and daughters; 14 And all the days of Cainan were 910 years, and he died. 15 And Mahlalael lived 65 years, and begot Jared; 16 And Mahlalael lived after he begot Jared 830 years, and begot sons and daughters. 17 And all the days of Mahlalael were 895 years, and he died. 18 And Jared lived 162 years, and begot Enoch. 19 And Jared lived after he begot Enoch 800 years, and begot sons and daughters; 20 And all the days of Jared were 962 years, and he died. 21 And Enoch lived 65 years, and begot Methuselah; 22 And Enoch found favor in the presence of God 300 years after he begot Methuselah, and begot sons and daughters; 23 And all the days of Enoch were 365 years; 24 And Enoch found favor in the presence of God, and disappeared; for God had took him away.

5:13
And Jared was 162 years old when he begat Enoch, which means Teacher/Initiated or Dedicated.

NOTE:
Not to be mistaken for Enoch, the Kenite, as in 4:17.

5:14
And Jared lived 800 years after the birth of Enoch. He fathered other sons and daughters and died at the age of 962.

5:15
And Enoch was 65 years old when he begat Methuselah, which means; A man of the javelin or It shall be sent.[the deluge]

5:16
And Enoch walked with Yahveh 300 years after the birth of Methuselah.

5:17
And Enoch lived a total of 365 years. Then Enoch was taken by Yahveh.

NOTE:
Meaning he did not die, but was taken up, just as Elijah was in II Kings 2:9-11.

5:18
And Methuselah was 187 years old when he begat Lamech, which means; Powerful/ Overthrower or A strong young man.

5:19
And Methuselah lived 782 years after the birth of Lamech. He fathered other sons and daughters, and died at the age of 969; the oldest man who ever lived.

NOTE:
Not to be mistaken for Lamech; the Kenite, as in 4:18.

28 And Lamech lived 182 years, and begat a son: 29 And he called his name Noah, saying, This same shall comfort us concerning our work and toil of our hands, because of the ground which the Lord hath cursed. 30 And Lamech lived after he begat Noah 595 years, and begat sons and daughters: 31 And all the days of Lamech were 777 years: and he died. 32 And Noah was 500 years old: and Noah begat Shem, Ham, and Japheth. 6:1 And it came to pass, when men began to multiply on the face of the earth, and daughters were born unto them. 2 That the sons of God saw the daughters of men that they were fair; and they took them wives of all they chose.

28 When Lamech had lived 182 years, he became the father of a son, 29 and called his name Noah, saying, "Out of the ground which the Lord has cursed this one shall bring us relief from our work and from the toil of our hands." 30 Lamech lived after the birth of Noah 595 years, and had other sons and daughters. 31 Thus all the days of Lamech were 777 years; and he died. 32 When Noah had lived 500 years, Noah begot Shem, Ham, and Japheth. 6:1 When men began to multiply on the face of the ground, and daughters were born to them, 2 the sons of God saw that the daughters of men were fair; and they took to wife such of them as they chose.

28 When Lamech had lived 182 years, he begot a son. 29 And he named him Noah, saying, "This one will provide us relief from our work and from the toil of our hands, out of the very soil which the Lord placed under a curse." 30 After the birth of Noah, Lamech lived 595 years and begot sons and daughters. 31 All the days of Lamech came to 777 years; then he died. 6:1 When men began to increase on the earth and daughters were born to them, 2 the divine beings saw how beautiful the daughters of men were and took wives from among those that pleased them.

28 And Lamech lived 182 years, and begot a son; 29 And he called his name Noah, saying, This one shall comfort us concerning our work and the toil of our hands, because of the ground which the Lord has cursed. 30 And Lamech lived after he begot Noah 595 years, and begot sons and daughters. 31 And all the days of Lamech were 777 years, and he died. 32 And Noah was 500 years old, and Noah begot Shem, Ham, and Japheth. 6:1 And it came to pass, when men began to multiply on the face of the earth and daughters were born to them, 2 That the sons of God saw that the daughters of men were fair; so they took them wives of all whom they chose.

19 Jared lived 800 years after the birth of Hanok, and was the father of sons and daughters. 20 Thus Jared lived for 962 years in all; then he died. 21 After living 65 years Hanok became the father of Methuselah. 22 For 300 years Hanok lived close to God, after the birth of Methuselah, and was the father of sons and daughters. 23 Thus Hanok lived for 365 years in all; Hanok lived close to God, and then he disappeared, for God took him away. 25 After living 187 years Methuselah became the father of Lemek; 26 Methuselah lived 782 years after the birth of Lemek, and was the father of sons and daughters. 27 Thus Methuselah lived for 969 years in all; then he died. 28 After living 182 years Lemek became the father of a son, 29 whom he called Noah, saying, "Now we shall 'know a' relief from our labour and from our toil on the ground that the Eternal cursed." 30 Lemek lived 595 years after the birth of Noah, and was the father of sons and daughters. 31 Thus Lemek lived 777 years in all; then he died. 32 After living 500 years Noah became the father of Shem, Ham, and Japheth. 6:1 Now when men began to multiply over all the world and had daughters born to them, 2 the angels noticed that the daughters of men were beautiful, and they married any one of them that they chose.

5:20
And Lamech was 182 years old when he begat Noah; which means, Rest/Comfort or Consolation. [a play on the statement, "This same shall give us rest.]

5:21
And Lamech lived 595 years after the birth of Noah. He fathered other sons and daughters, and died at the age of 777. ^{v.2:3}

5:22
And by the time Noah was 500 years old, he had three sons.

1st: Japheth meaning; Beauty/Let him enlarge, or He that persuades.

2nd: Ham meaning; Swarthy.

3rd: Shem meaning; Renown

CHAPTER SIX
6:1
And it came to pass, that when Adam's family grew and began to multiply in the land, that daughters were born unto them. [Adam & Eve]

6:2
And the angels saw that the daughters of Adam were very beautiful, and the temptation and lust for them grew so strong that some angels; provoked by Lucifer, left Heaven and came down to Earth, and had sexual intercourse with anyone of them that they chose.

NOTE:
Shem, the youngest, had the family blessings.

NOTE:
Chapter 5 was the genealogy of Adam up to Noah. Chapter 6 verses 1-3 goes back to the time of Adam.

NOTE:
Jude 6
And the angels which kept not their first estate, but left their own HABITATION, [heaven] (God has them now) HE HATH RESERVED in everlasting chains (until) under darkness UNTO the JUDGMENT OF THE GREAT DAY.

NOTE:
The angels in v.6:2 are called (morning stars) "THE FALLEN ANGELS." 7,000 of the one third, deceived by Lucifer as written in Rev. 12:4-9.

3 And the Lord said, My spirit shall not always strive with man, for that he also is flesh: yet his days shall be an hundred and twenty years. 4 There were giants in the earth in those days; and also after that, when the sons of God came in unto the daughters of men, and they bare children to them, the same became mighty men which were of old, men of renown.

3 Then the Lord said, "My spirit shall not abide in man for ever, for he is flesh, but his days shall be a hundred and twenty years." 4 The Nephilim were on the earth in those days, and also afterward, when the sons of God came in to the daughters of men, and they bore children to them. These were the mighty men that were of old, the men of renown.

3 The Lord said, "My breath shall not abide in man forever, since he too is flesh; let the days allowed him be one hundred and twenty years." 4 It was then, and later too, that the Nephilim appeared on earth—when the divine beings cohabited with the daughters of men, who bore them offspring. They were the heroes of old, the men of renown.

3 Then the Lord said, My spirit shall not dwell in man forever, because he is flesh; let his days be a hundred and twenty years. 4 There were giants on the earth in those days; and also after that, for the sons of God came in unto the daughters of men, and they bore children to them, and they became giants who in the olden days were mighty men of renown.

3 So the Eternal said, "Human creatures are but flesh; my spirit is not to be immortal in them; they shall not live more than a hundred and twenty years." 4 (It was in these days that the Nephilim giants arose on the earth, as well as afterwards whenever angels had intercourse with the daughters of men and had children born to them; these were the heroes who were famous in the days of old.) 5 When the Eternal saw that the wickedness of man on earth was great, and that man's mind was never bent on anything but evil, 6 the Eternal was sorry that he had ever made man on the earth; it was a grief to him. 7 So the Eternal said, "I will blot him off the earth, this man that I have formed—man and beast and reptile and bird; I am sorry that I ever made them." 8 However, Noah had found favour with the Eternal.9 Here are the descendants of Noah. Noah was an upright man, blameless among the men of his day; Noah lived close to God. 10 Noah was the father of three sons, Shem, Ham, and Japheth. 11 Now in God's sight the earth was corrupt, the earth was full of insolence and outrage; 12 God saw that the earth was corrupt, for every human being upon earth had corrupted his life.

6:3

And the Lord said,"My spirit shall not always remain in Adam, for he is flesh. So the number of years remaining in his life shall be 120.

6:4

As the **FALLEN ANGELS** continued threw the years to have sexual intercourse with the daughters of men, the offspring of these conceptions produced Giant, Mighty Men, with supernatural powers, and were given spiritual knowledge about the heavens and the world that then was. These giants were the reason for the flood of Noah, but there was also a second influx of these giants after the flood.

NOTE:
Many times Angels and Satan himself are referred to as a man or son of God.

NOTE:
John 3:6
That which is born of the flesh is flesh; and that which is born of the spirit is spirit.

Whether one is of flesh, or one is of spirit, we are all SONS OF GOD.

* *

SCRIPTURE STUDY #3
SONS OF GOD = ANGELS/PEOPLE

A) Isaiah 14:16
B) Ezek. 28:2,9
C) Job 1:6 2:1 38:7
D) Psalm 29:1   (mighty = angels)
      89:6   (sons of the mighty = angels)
E) Daniel 3:25
F) Gen. 19   [read the whole chapter]
G) For more knowledge about Lucifer and his fall,
   read the entire chapters of:
                    1) Isaiah 14
                    2) Ezek. 28:1-19
                    3) Rev. 12
                    4) Jude

5 And God saw that the wickedness of man was great in the earth, and that every imagination of the thoughts of his heart was only evil continually.6 And it repented the Lord that he had made man on the earth, and it grieved him at his heart. 7 And the Lord said, I will destroy man whom I have created from the face of the earth; both man, and beast, and the creeping thing, and the fowls of the air; for it repenteth me that I have made them. 8 But Noah found grace in the eyes of the Lord. 9 These are the generations of Noah: Noah was a just man and perfect in his generations, and Noah walked with God. 10 And Noah begat three sons, Shem, Ham, and Japheth. 11 The earth also was corrupt before God, and the earth was filled with violence.

5 The Lord saw that the wickedness of man was great in the earth, and that every imagination of the thoughts of his heart was only evil continually. 6 And the Lord was sorry that he had made man on the earth, and it grieved him to his heart. 7 So the Lord said, "I will blot out man whom I have created from the face of the ground, man and beast and creeping things and birds of the air, for I am sorry that I have made them." 8 But Noah found favor in the eyes of the Lord.9 These are the generations of Noah. Noah was a righteous man, blameless in his generation; Noah walked with God. 10 And Noah had three sons, Shem, Ham, and Japheth. 11 Now the earth was corrupt in God's sight, and the earth was filled with violence.

5 The Lord saw how great was man's wickedness on earth, and how every plan devised by his mind was nothing but evil all the time. 6 And the Lord regretted that He had made man on earth, and His heart was saddened. 7 The Lord said, "I will blot out from the earth the men whom I created—men together with beast, creeping things, and birds of the sky; for I regret that I made them." 8 But Noah found favor with the Lord. 9 This is the line of Noah.— Noah was a righteous man; he was blameless in his age; Noah walked with God.—10 Noah begot three sons: Shem, Ham, and Japheth. 11 The earth became corrupt before God; the earth was filled with lawlessness. 12 When God saw how corrupt the earth was, for all flesh had corrupted its ways on earth,

5 And the Lord saw that the wickedness of man was great in the earth, and that every imagination of the thoughts of his heart was evil continually. 6 And the Lord was sorry that he had made man on the earth, and it grieved him in his heart. 7 So the Lord said, I will destroy men whom I have created from the face of the earth; both men and animals, and the creeping things, and the fowls of the air; I am sorry that I have made them. 8 But Noah found mercy in the eyes of the Lord. 9 These are the generations of Noah: Noah was a just man and innocent in his days, and God was pleased with Noah. 10 And Noah begot three sons, Shem, Ham, and Japheth. 11 The earth was corrupt in the presence of God, and the earth was filled with wickedness.

6:5
   And God saw that the wickedness of man

had greatly multiplied, and that every

thought of the imagination, purpose, and

desire of man was perverse and evil

continually every day.

6:6
   And it repented the Lord that he had

made man.

6:7   (blot out)
   And the Lord said,"I will **DESTROY** the
                                           v.4
NEPHILIUM and all the men, women, and

children that live and partake of the

evil that flourish in this part of the

world. And all that lives and exist

around them, I will also wipe off the

face of the Earth."

6:8
   But Noah walked with, and found grace

in the eyes of the Lord.

6:9
   Noah and his family were the only

generation of Adam still found to have

a perfect pedigree.

6:10
   Noah and his sons, Japheth, Ham,

and Shem had not inter-mixed with the

NEPHILIM.

12 And God looked upon the earth, and, behold, it was corrupt; for all flesh had corrupted his way upon the earth. 13 And God said unto Noah, The end of all flesh is come before me; for the earth is filled with violence through them; and behold, I will destroy them with the earth. 14 Make thee an ark of gopher wood; rooms shalt thou make in the ark, and shalt pitch it within and without pitch. 15 And this is the fashion which thou shalt make it of: The length of the ark shall be 300 cubits, the breadth of it 50 cubits, and the height of it 30 cubits. 16 A window shalt thou make to the ark, and in a cubit shalt thou finish it above; and the door of the ark shalt thou set in the side thereof; with lower, second, and third stories shalt thou make it.

12 And God saw the earth, and behold, it was corrupt; for all flesh had corrupted their way upon the earth. 13 And God said to Noah, "I have determined to make an end of all flesh; for the earth is filled with violence through them; behold, I will destroy them with the earth. 14 Make yourself an ark of gopher wood; make rooms in the ark, and cover it inside and out with pitch. 15 This is how you are to make it: the length of the ark 300 cubits, its breadth 50 cubits, and its height 30 cubits. 16 Make a roof for the ark, and finish it to a cubit above; and set the door of the ark in its side; make it with lower, second, and third decks.

12 When God saw how corrupt the earth was, for all flesh had corrupted its ways on earth, 13 God said to Noah, "I have decided to put an end to all flesh, for the earth is filled with lawlessness because of them: I am about to destroy them with the earth. 14 Make yourself an ark of gopher wood; make it an ark with compartments, and cover it inside and out with pitch. 15 This is how you shall make it: the length of the ark shall be 300 cubits, its width 50 cubits, and its height 30 cubits. 16 Make an opening for daylight in the ark, and terminate it within a cubit of the top. Put the entrance to the ark in its side; make it with bottom, second, and third decks.

12 And God saw that the earth was corrupt; for all flesh had corrupted its way upon the earth. 13 So God said to Noah, The end of all flesh is come before me; for the earth is full of wickedness through men; and, behold, I will destroy them with the earth. 14 Make yourself an ark of gopher wood; make rooms in the ark and daub it without and within with pitch. 15 And this is how you shall make it: the length of the ark shall be 300 cubits, the breadth of it 50 cubits, and the height of it 30 cubits. 16 And you shall make a window in the ark, and to the width of a cubit shall you finish it above; and the door of the ark you shall make in its side; with lower, second, and third decks you shall make it.

13 So God said to Noah, "I have resolved to put an end to every human being, for they have filled the earth with insolence and outrage; I will destroy them and the earth together.14 Build a barge of cypress wood, build cabins inside the barge, and cover it with pitch, inside and outside. 15 This is how you are to build it: the barge is to be 450' long, 75' broad, and 40' high. 16 you must put windows in the barge, 18" from the roof, and make a door in the side of the barge; also put three decks in it. 17 For I am sending a deluge of water on the earth, to destroy every living creature under heaven; every thing on earth shall perish.

6:11
This part of the Earth was filled with violence and was wasting away.

6:12
And Yahveh looked upon this part of the Earth, and behold, the Earth was waste and all flesh had inter-mixed with the Nephilim except Noah and his family.

6:13
And Yahveh said to Noah, "The end of all flesh is come before Me. For this part of the Earth is filled with violence. I will destroy all the life living here from then face of the Earth.

6:14
Build an **ARK** of gopher wood with many rooms, and coat the Ark inside and out with resin.

6:15
The length of the ark shall be 300 cubits and the height of the ark shall be 30 cubits.

6:16
The inside of the ark shall have a lower level, and two upper levels. A door shall you set in the side of the. And to allow light in, you shall build a window on the top of the ark.

COMMENT:
If Lucifer and his Fallen Angels had inter-mixed with Noah and his sons, Satan would have successfully defeated Yahveh by stopping the perfect pedigree of Adam's generations; thus Yahshua would not have been born of Adam, but would have been born of Cain; Satan's offspring. But as we all know; Yahshua was born of Adam's generations thus defeating Satan and in the very near future; completely destroying him and all his followers.

17 And, behold, I, even I, do bring a flood of waters upon the earth, to destroy all flesh, wherein is the breath of life, from under heaven; and every thing that is in the earth shall die.18 But with thee will I establish my covenant; and thou shalt come into the ark, thou, and thy sons, and thy wife, and thy sons' wives with thee. 19 And of every living thing of all flesh, two of every sort shalt thou bring into the ark, to keep them alive with thee; they shall be male and female. 20 Of fowls after their kind, of cattle after their kind, of every creeping thing of the earth after his kind, two of every sort shall come unto thee, to keep them alive. 21 And take thou unto thee of all the food that is eaten, and thou shalt gather it to thee; and it shall be for food for thee, and for them. 22 Thus did Noah; according to all that God commanded him, so he did. 7:1 And the Lord said unto Noah, Come thou and all thy house into the ark; for thee have I seen righteous before me in this generation.

17 For behold, I will bring a flood of waters upon the earth, to destroy all flesh in which is the breath of life from under heaven; everything that is on the earth shall die. 18 But I will establish my covenant with you; and you shall come into the ark, you, your sons, your wife, and your sons' wives with you. 19 And of every living thing of all flesh, you shall bring two of every sort into the ark, to keep them alive with you; they shall be male and female. 20 Of the birds according to their kinds, and of the animals according to their kinds, of every creeping thing of the ground according to its kind, two of every sort shall come in to you, to keep them alive. 21 Also take with you every sort of food that is eaten, and store it up; and it shall serve as food for you and for them." 22 Noah did this; he did all that God commanded him. 7:1 Then the Lord said unto Noah, "Go into the ark, you and all your household, for I have seen that you are righteous before me in this generation.

17 For My part, I am about to bring the Flood—waters upon the earth—to destroy all flesh under the sky in which there is the breath of life; everything on earth shall perish. 18 But I will establish My covenant with you, and you shall enter the ark, with your sons, your wife, and your sons' wives.19 And of all that lives, of all flesh, you shall take two of each into the ark to keep alive with you; they shall be male and female. 20 From birds of every kind, cattle of every kind, every kind of creeping thing on earth, two of each shall come to you to stay alive. 21 For your part, take of everything that is eaten and store it away, to serve as food for you and for them." 22 Noah did so; just as God commanded him, so he did. 7:1 Then the Lord said to Noah, "Go into the ark, with all your house-hold, for you alone have I found righteous before me in this generation.

17 And, behold, I will bring a flood of waters upon the earth, to destroy all flesh that has the breath of life in it from under heaven; and everything that is on the earth shall die. 18 But I will establish my covenant with you; and you shall enter into the ark, you, and your sons, and your wife, and your sons' wives with you.19 And of every living thing of all flesh, two of every kind bring into the ark, to keep them alive with you; they shall be male and female. 20 Of fowls after their kind, and of animals after their kind, and of every creeping thing of the earth after its kind, two of every kind shall enter with you, that they may live. 21 And you must take a supple of all food that is eaten, and you shall store it by you; and it shall be for food for you and for them. 22 Thus did Noah; according to all that God commanded him, so did he. 7:1 Then God said to Noah, Enter into the ark; you and all your household, for you alone have I seen righteous before me in this generation.

6:17

Behold, soon I will bring a flood of water upon this part of the Earth, and all that lives here shall die.

6:18

But with you Noah, I will establish my covenant. Into the ark shall you and your family go to escape the flood.

6:19

You shall also bring into the ark two of every living creature, one male and one female.

6:20

All the different species of birds, beasts, reptiles, and of every moving creature of the ground, shall you bring into the ark to keep them alive.

6:21

You shall also bring into the ark, all food that is eaten. It shall be for you and all the living creatures that are with you."

6:22

So Noah did everything Yahveh commanded him to do.

CHAPTER SEVEN
7:1

And Yahveh said unto Noah, "Bring your family into the ark, for in you I have seen righteousness.

2 Of every clean beast thou shalt take to thee by sevens, the male and his female: and of beasts that are not clean by two, the male and his female.3 Of fowls also of the air by sevens, the male and the female; to keep seed alive upon the face of all the earth. 4 For yet seven days, and I will cause it to rain upon the earth 40 days and 40 nights; and every living substance that I have made will I destroy from off the face of the earth.5 And Noah did according unto all that the Lord commanded him. 6 And Noah was 600 years old when the flood of waters was upon the earth. 7 And Noah went in, and his sons, and his wife, and his sons' wives with him, into the ark, because of the waters of the flood. 8 Of clean beasts, and of beasts that are not clean, and of fowls, and of every thing that creepeth upon the earth, 9 There went in two and two unto Noah into the ark, the male and the female, as God had commanded Noah.

2 Take with you seven pairs of all clean animals, the male and his mate; and a pair of animals that are not clean, the male and his mate;3 and seven pairs of the birds of the air also, male and female, to keep their kind alive upon the face of all the earth. 4 For in seven days I will send rain upon the earth 40 days and 40 nights; and every living thing that I have made I will blot out from the face of the ground." 5 And Noah did all that the Lord had commanded him. 6 Noah was 600 years old when the flood of waters came upon the earth. 7 And Noah and his sons and his wife and his sons' wives with him went into the ark, to escape the waters of the flood. 8 Of clean animals, and of animals that are not clean, and of birds, and of everything that creeps on the ground, 9 two by two, male and female, went into the ark with Noah, as God had commanded Noah.

2 Of every clean animal you shall take seven pairs, males and their mates, and of every animal that is not clean, two, male and its mate;3 of the birds of the sky also, seven pairs, male and female, to keep seed alive upon all the earth. 4 For in seven days' time I will make it rain upon the earth, 40 days and 40 nights, and I will blot out from the earth all existence that I created." 5 And Noah did just as the Lord commanded him. 6 Noah was 600 years old when the Flood came, waters upon the earth. 7 Noah, with his sons, his wife, and his sons' wives, went into the ark because of the waters of the flood. 8 Of the clean animals, of the animals that are not clean, of the birds, and of everything that creeps on the ground, 9 two of each, male and female, came to Noah into the ark, as God had commanded Noah.

2 Of all clean animals you shall take with you seven pairs, both males and females; and of the beasts that are not clean two pairs, males and females. 3 Likewise, of the fowls of the air that are clean seven pairs, both males and females; to keep their posterity alive upon the face of the earth. 4 For in seven days I will cause it to rain upon the earth 40 days and 40 nights; and every living thing that I have made will I destroy from off the face of the earth. 5 And Noah did according to all that the Lord commanded him. 6 And Noah was 600 years old when the flood of waters came upon the earth. 7 And Noah, with his sons and his wife and his sons' wives, went into the ark because of the waters of the flood. 8 Of clean animals, and of unclean animals, and of fowls, and of everything that creeps upon the earth, 9 There went in two and two with Noah into the ark, the males and the females, as God had commanded Noah.

18 But I will make a compact of my own with you; you shall enter the barge, you and your sons and your wife and your sons' wives along with you. 19 And you shall take into the barge, two living creatures of every kind, to keep them along with you; one is to be a male, and one a female.

7:2
   And of all clean beasts bring in seven
pairs. [these animals will be used for
sacrifices] And of all unclean beasts
bring in one male and one female.

7:3
   And of all birds, bring in seven pairs
so that their seed may remain alive after
the flood.

7:4
   For in seven days I will cause it to
rain down water forty days and forty
nights. And every living creature of this
part of the Earth will I blot out of
existence."

7:5
   And Noah did all that Yahveh commanded
him to do

7:6
   And Noah was 600 years old when the
flood of water came down upon the Earth.

7:7
   And Noah, his wife, and his sons and
their wives went into the ark.

7:8,9
   And all the animals; which Yahveh
commanded Noah to take into the ark,
went in two by two, one female, one male.

NOTE:
#40 = probation.

NOTE:
#600 = warfare.

10 And it came to pass after seven days, that the waters of the flood were upon the earth. 11 In the 600th year of Noah's life, in the second month, the seventeenth day of the month, the same day were all the fountains of the great deep broken up, and the windows of heaven were opened. 12 And the rain was upon the earth 40 days and 40 nights. 13 In the selfsame day entered Noah, and Shem, and Ham, and Japheth, the sons of Noah, and Noah's wife, and the three wives of his sons with them, into the ark; 14 They, and every beast after his kind, and all the cattle after their kind, and every creeping thing that creepeth upon the earth after his kind, and every fowl after his kind, every bird of every sort. 15 And they went in unto Noah into the ark, two and two of all flesh, wherein is the breath of life. 16 And they that went in, went in male and female of all flesh, as God had commanded him: and the Lord shut him in.

10 And after seven days the waters of the flood came upon the earth. 11 In the 600th year of Noah's life, in the second month, on the 17th day of the month, on that day all the fountains of the great deep burst forth, and the windows of the heavens were opened. 12 And rain fell upon the earth 40 days and 40 nights. 13 On the very same day Noah and his sons, Shem and Ham and Japheth, and Noah's wife and the three wives of his sons with them entered the ark, 14 they and every beast according to its kind, and all the cattle according to their kinds, and every creeping thing that creeps on the earth according to its kind, and every bird according to its kind, every bird of every sort. 15 They went into the ark with Noah, two and two of all flesh in which there was the breath of life. 16 And they that entered, male and female of all flesh, went in as God had commanded him; and the Lord shut him in.

.10 And on the seventh day the waters of the flood came upon the earth. 11 In the 600th year of Noah's life, in the second month, on the 17th day of the month, on that day All the fountains of the great deep burst apart, And all the floodgates of the sky broke open. (12 The rain fell on the earth 40 days and 40 nights.) 13 That same day Noah and Noah's sons, Shem, Ham, and Japheth, went into the ark, with Noah's wife and the three wives of his sons—14 they and all beasts of every kind, all cattle of every kind, all creatures of every kind that creep on the earth, and all birds of every kind, every bird, every winged thing. 15 They came to Noah into the ark, two each of all flesh in which there was breath of life. 16 Thus they that entered comprised male and female of all flesh, as God had commanded him. And the Lord shut him in.

10 And it came to pass after seven days that the waters of the flood came upon the earth. 11 In the 600th year of Noah's life, in the second month, the 17th day of the month, on that very day all the fountains of the great deep burst forth and the windows of heaven were opened. 12 And the rain fell upon the earth for 40 days and 40 nights. 13 On that same day entered Noah and Shem and Ham and Japheth, the sons of Noah, and Noah's wife, and the three wives of his sons with him, into the ark; 14 They and every beast after its kind and all the cattle after their kind and every creeping thing that creeps upon the earth after its kind and every fowl after its kind, every bird of every sort. 15 They went with Noah into the ark, two and two of all flesh in which there is the breath of life. 16 And they that entered, males and females of every living thing went in, as God had commanded him. Then the Lord shut him in.

20 Two of every kind, bird, beast, and reptile, are to join you, that they may be kept alive. 21 Go and gather anything in the shape of food, to be food for you and for them." 22 Noah did so; he did all that God had ordered him.

7:10
    And it came to pass, after seven
v.1:6-8
days, that the **WATERS OF HEAVEN** rained

down upon the Earth.

NOTE:
(about 2347 B.C.)
also the first time
it has ever rained
on the Earth.

7:11
    And in the 600th year of Noah's life,

on the 17th day of the 2nd month,
v.1:6
Yahveh broke open the **EXPANSE** and the
v.1:8
FIRMAMENT rained down through the
(windows of heaven)
HEAVENLY FLOODGATES.

7:12
    This was the first day of the

great deluge.

7:13
    In that same day, Noah and his family

went into the ark.

7:14
    Also every living creature after its

own kind went into the ark.

7:15
    And they all went passed Noah into

the ark, two by two, of all flesh in

which was the breath of life.

NOTE:
I Cor. 15:39
All flesh is not the
same flesh: but there
is one kind of flesh
of men, another flesh
of beasts, another of
fishes, and another of
birds.

7:16
    And when everyone, and every living

creature was in the ark, **YAHVEH** closed

the door and shut them in.

17 And the flood was 40 days upon the earth; and the waters increased, and bare up the ark, and it was lifted up above the earth. 18 And the waters prevailed, and were increased greatly upon the earth; and the ark went upon the face of the waters. 19 And the waters prevailed exceedingly upon the earth; and all the high hills, that were under the whole heaven, were covered. 20 Fifteen cubits upward did the waters prevail; and the mountains were covered. 21 And all flesh died that moved upon the earth, both fowl, and of cattle, and of beast, and of every creeping thing that creepeth upon the earth, and every man: 22 All in whose nostrils was the breath of life, of all that was in the dry land, died.23 And every living substance was destroyed which was upon the face of the ground, both man, and cattle, and the creeping things, and the fowl of the heaven; and they were destroyed from the earth: and Noah only remained alive, and they that were with him in the ark. 24 And the waters prevailed upon the earth 150 days.

17 The flood continued 40 days upon the earth; and the waters increased, and bore up the ark, and it rose high above the earth. 18 The waters prevailed and increased greatly upon the earth; and the ark floated on the face of the waters. 19 And the waters prevailed so mightily upon the earth that all the high mountains under the whole heaven were covered; 20 the waters prevailed above the mountains, covering them 15 cubits deep. 21 And all flesh died that moved upon the earth, birds, cattle, beasts, all swarming creatures that swarm upon the earth, and every man; 22 everything on the dry land in whose nostrils was the breath of life died.23 He blotted out every living thing that was upon the face of the ground, man and animals and creeping things and birds of the air; they were blotted out from the earth. Only Noah was left, and those that were with him in the ark. 24 And the waters prevailed upon the earth 150 days.

17 The flood continued 40 days on the earth, and the waters increased and raised the ark so that it rose above the earth. 18 The waters swelled and increased greatly upon the earth, and the ark drifted upon the waters. 19 When the waters had swelled much more upon the earth, all the highest mountains everywhere under the sky were covered. 20 15 cubits higher did the waters swell, as the mountains were covered. 21 And all flesh that stirred on the earth perished—birds, cattle, beasts, and all the things that swarmed upon the earth, and all mankind. 22 All in whose nostrils was the merest breath of life, all that was on dry land, died.23 All existence on earth was blotted out—man, cattle, creeping things, and birds of the sky; they were blotted out from the earth. Only Noah was left, and those with him in the ark. 24 And when the waters had swelled on the earth 150 days,

17 And the flood lasted 40 days upon the earth; and the waters increased and bore up the ark so that it was lifted up above the earth. 18 And the waters prevailed and rose higher upon the earth; and the ark floated on the face of the waters. 19 And the waters prevailed exceedingly upon the earth; so that all the high mountains under the whole heaven were covered. 20 15 cubits above the mountains did the waters prevail; and the mountains were covered. 21 And all flesh died that moved upon the earth, both of fowl and of cattle and of wild beast and of every creeping thing that creeps upon the earth and every man; 22 Everything in whose nostrils was the breath of life, of all that was on the dry land, died. 23 And every living thing was destroyed that was upon the face of the ground, both man and animals and the creeping things and the fowl of the air; they were destroyed from the earth; and Noah only remained, and those who were with him in the ark. 24 And the waters prevailed upon the earth 150 days.

7:17
   And it rained down water forty days
and forty nights creating a great flood.
And as the waters increased the ark was
lifted up off the Earth.

7:18
   And the waters prevailed exceedingly
upon the Earth. And the ark floated upon
the face of the waters.

7:19
   And the waters prevailed exceedingly
upon this part of the Earth, and all the
high hills were covered.

7:20
   Fifteen cubits upward did the waters
prevail; and the mountains were covered.

7:21
   And all flesh died that lived in
this part of the Earth; every bird, beast,
reptile, and creature, including man.

7:22
   All flesh in whose nostrils was the
breath of life, and lived on the dry land
perished.

7:23
   Every living substance which lived in
this part of the Earth, was destroyed. Only
Noah and his family, and all the creatures
with him in the ark remained alive.

7:24
   And the waters prevailed upon the Earth
150 days.

NOTE:
This is a 5
month period
of destruction,
just like the 5
month period of
destruction Satan
will bring to the
Earth in the near
future.

Rev. 12:15
   (Satan)
And the SERPENT
cast out of his
   (lies)
mouth WATER as a
flood after the
(Isreal)
 WOMAN, that he
might cause her to
   (deceived because)
be CARRIED AWAY of
the flood.(of lies)

8:1 And God remembered Noah, and every living thing, and all the cattle that was with him in the ark: and God made a wind to pass over the earth, and the waters assuaged; 2 The fountains also of the deep and the windows of heaven were stopped, and the rain from heaven was restrained;3 And the waters returned from off the earth continually: and after the end of the 150 days the waters were abated. 4 And the ark rested in the seventh month, on the seventeenth day of the month, upon the mountains of Ararat. 5 And the waters decreased continually until the tenth month: in the tenth month, on the first day of the month, were the tops of the mountains seen. 6 And it came to pass at the end of 40 days, that Noah opened the window of the ark which he had made:

8:1 But God remembered Noah and all the beasts and all the cattle that were with him in the ark. And God made a wind blow over the earth, and the waters subsided; 2 the fountains of the deep and the windows of the heavens were closed, the rain from the heavens was restrained,3 and the waters receded from the earth continually. At the end of 150 days the waters had abated; 4 and in the seventh month, on the seventeenth day of the month, the ark came to rest upon the mountains of Ararat. 5 And the waters continued to abate until the tenth month; in the tenth month, on the first day of the month, the tops of the mountains were seen. 6 At the end of 40 days Noah opened the window of the ark which he had made,

8:1 God remembered Noah and all the beasts and all the cattle that were with him in the ark, and God caused a wind to blow across the earth, and the waters subsided. 2 The fountains of the deep and the flood-gates of the sky were stopped up, and the rain from the sky was held back;3 the waters receded steadily from the earth. At the end of 150 days the waters diminished, 4 so that in the seventh month, on the seventeenth day of the month, the ark came to rest on the mountains or Ararat. 5 The waters went on diminishing until the tenth month; in the tenth month. on the first of the month, the tops of the mountains became visible. 6 At the end of 40 days, Noah opened the window of the ark that he had made

8:1 And God remembered Noah and every living thing and all the animals and all the fowls that were with him in the ark; and God made a wind to blow over the earth, and the waters became calm; 2 The fountains of the deep and the windows of heaven were closed, and the rain from the sky was restrained; 3 And the waters receded from the earth gradually; and after 150 days the waters abated. 4 And in the seventh month, on the seventeenth day of the month, the ark rested on the mountains of Kardo. 5 And the waters decreased gradually until the tenth month; on the first day of the tenth month, the tops of the mountains were seen. 6 And it came to pass at the end of 40 days that Noah opened the window of the ark which he had made;

7:1 Then said the Eternal to Noah, "Go into the barge, you and all your household, for I have adjudged you, among all the men of to-day, to be upright before me. 2 Take seven pairs, male and female, of every clean animal, and one pair, male and female, of the unclean animals, 3 and seven pairs, male and female, of the birds of the air, to maintain life over all the world. 4 For after seven days I will make it rain on earth for 40 days and 40 nights, and I will blot off the earth every living creature that I ever made." 5 Noah did all that the Eternal ordered him. 6 Noah was 600 years old when the deluge of water flooded the earth. 7 and Noah went into the barge along with his sons and his wife and his sons' wives, driven by the waters of the deluge. 8 Pairs of animals clean and unclean, of birds and of reptiles, 9 male and female, accompanied Noah into the barge, as God had ordered Noah.

CHAPTER EIGHT

8:1
    And Yahveh remembered Noah, and all
the living creatures with him in the ark.
And the Holy Spirit of God passed over the
Earth, and the waters started to recede.

8:2   v.7:11
    So the **HEAVENLY FLOODGATES** were now
                 v.1:6-8
closed and the **WATERS OF HEAVEN** no longer
rained down upon the Earth.

8:3
    And the waters receded from off the
Earth continually: and after 150 days
had passed, the waters were decreasing.

8:4
    And the ark rested in the 7th month,
on the 17th day of that month, upon the
mountains of Ararat.

8:5
    And the waters decreased continually
until the 10th month. In the 10th month
on the first day of that month, were the
tops of the mountains seen.

8:6
    Forty days later Noah opened the
window of the ark.

7 And sent forth a raven, which went forth to and fro, until the waters were dried up from off the earth. 8 Also he sent forth a dove from the him, to see if the waters were abated from off the face of the ground; 9 But the dove found no rest for the sole of her foot, and she returned unto him into the ark, for the waters were on the face of the whole earth: then he put forth his hand, and took her, and pulled her in unto him into the ark. 10 And stayed yet other seven days; and again he sent forth the dove out of the ark; 11 And the dove came in to him in the evening; and, lo, in her mouth was an olive leaf plucked off: so Noah knew that the waters were abated from off the earth. 12 And he stayed yet another seven days; and sent forth the dove; which returned not again unto him any more. **RSV**

7 and sent forth a raven; and it went to and fro until the waters were dried up from the earth. 8 Then he sent forth a dove from him, to see if the waters had subsided from the face of the ground; 9 but the dove found no place to set her foot, and she returned to him to the ark, for the waters were still on the face of the whole earth. So he put forth his hand and took her and brought her into the ark with him. 10 He waited another seven days, and again he sent forth the dove out of the ark; 11 and the dove came back to him in the evening, and lo, in her mouth a freshly plucked olive leaf; so Noah knew that the waters had subsided from the earth. 12 Then he waited another seven days, and sent forth the dove; and she did not return to him any more.

7 and sent out the raven; it went to and fro until the waters had dried up from the earth. 8 Then he sent out the dove to see whether the waters had decreased from the surface of the ground. 9 But he dove could not find a resting place for its foot, and returned to him to the ark, for there was water over all the earth. So putting out his hand, he took it into the ark with him. 10 He waited another seven days, and again sent out the dove from the ark. 11 The dove came back to him toward evening, and there in its bill was a plucked-off olive leaf! Then Noah knew that the waters had decreased on the earth. 12 He waited still another seven days and sent the dove forth; and it did not return to him any more. **HOLY BIBLE GNL**

7 And he sent forth a raven which went to and fro, but did not return until the waters were dried up from the face of the earth. 8 Then he sent forth a dove from the ark, to see if the waters had abated from the face of the ground;
9 But the dove found no resting place for her foot, and she returned to him in the ark, for the waters were still on the face of the whole earth. Then he put forth his hand, and took her, and brought her into the ark with him.
10 And he waited yet another seven days; and again he sent forth the dove out of the ark; 11 And the dove came back to him in the evening; and, lo, in her mouth was an olive leaf plucked off; so Noah knew that the waters had subsided from off the earth. 12 And he waited another seven days, and sent forth the dove; but the dove did not return again to him any more.

10 At the end of the seven days, the waters of the deluge covered the earth. 11 In the 600th year of Noah's life, in the second month, on the 17th day of the month, on that day the fountains of the great abyss all burst, and the sluices of heaven were opened; 12 For 40 days and 40 nights rain fell upon the earth; 13 on that very day Noah, with Shem and Ham and Japheth, Noah's sons, and Noah's wife, and the three wives of his sons, went into the barge, with every kind of beast, with every kind of animal, with every reptile that crawls on the earth, and with every kind of bird and winged creature; 15 they accompanied Noah into the barge, pairs of every living creature, male and female, entering, as God had ordered him. 16 Then the Eternal shut him in.

8:7
And he sent forth a **RAVEN,** which flew here and there, and returned not unto the ark.

8:8
Noah also sent forth a **DOVE** from the ark, to see if the waters had receded off the face of the ground.

8:9
But the dove found no rest for the sole of her foot, and as she returned, Noah put forth his hand, and took her, and brought her in unto himself, and then into the ark.

8:10
And Noah patiently waited another seven days, and again he sent forth the dove out of the ark.

8:11
And the dove came into him in the evening: and surprisingly unto Noah, in her mouth was a plucked off, newly sprouted olive leaf: so Noah knew that the waters were decreasing from the Earth.

8:12
And Noah waited yet another seven days: and sent forth the dove, which returned not again to him anymore.

13 And it came to pass in the 601 year, in the first month, the first day of the month, the waters were dried up from off the earth: and Noah removed the covering of the ark, and looked, and behold, the face of the ground was dry. 14 And in the second month, on the 27th day of the month, was the earth dried. 15 And God spoke unto Noah, saying, 16 Go forth of the ark, thou, and thy wife, and thy sons, and thy sons' wives with thee. 17 Bring forth with thee every living thing that is with thee, of all flesh, both of fowl, and of cattle, and of every creeping thing that creepeth upon the earth; that they may breed abundantly in the earth, and be fruitful, and multiply upon the earth. 18 And Noah went forth, and his sons, and his wife, and his sons' wives with him. 19 Every beast, every creeping thing, and every fowl, and what-soever creepeth upon the earth, after their kinds, went forth out of the ark.

13 In the 601 year, in the first month, the first day of the month, the waters were dried from off the earth; and Noah removed the covering of the ark, and looked, and behold, the face of the ground was dry. 14 In the second month, on the 27th day of the month, the earth was dry. 15 Then God said to Noah, 16 "Go forth from the ark, you and your wife, and your sons and your sons' wives with you.17 Bring forth with you every living thing that is with you of all flesh—birds and animals and every creeping thing that creeps on the earth—that they may breed abundantly on the earth, and be fruitful and multiply upon the earth." 18 So Noah went forth, and his sons and his wife and his sons' wives with him. 19 And every beast, every creeping thing, and every bird, everything that moves upon the earth, went forth by families out of the ark.

13 In the 601 year, in the first month, on the first of the month, the waters began to dry from the earth; and when Noah removed the covering of the ark, he saw that the surface of the ground was drying. 14 And in the second month, on the 27th day of the month, the earth was dry. 15 God spoke to Noah, saying, 16 "Come out of the ark, together with your wife, your sons, and your sons' wives.17 Bring out with you every living thing of all flesh that is with you: birds, animals, and everything that creeps on earth; and let them swarm on the earth and be fertile and increase on earth." 18 So Noah came out, together with his sons, his wife, and his sons' wives. 19 Every animal, every creeping thing, and every bird, everything that stirs on earth came out of the ark by families.

13 And it came to pass in the 601 year, in the first month, the first day of the month, the waters were dried up from off the earth; and Noah removed the covering of the ark, and looked, and, behold, the face of the ground was dry. 14 And in the second month, on the 27th day of the month, the earth was dry. 15 And God spoke to Noah, saying, 16 Go forth out of the ark, you and your wife and your sons and your sons' wives with you.17 Bring forth with you every beast of every kind that si is with you, both fowl and cattle and every creeping thing that creeps on the earth; that they may breed abundantly on the earth and be fruitful and multiply upon the face of the earth. 18 So Noah went forth, and his sons and his wife and his sons' wives with him; 19 Every beast, every domestic animal, and every fowl, and whatever creeps upon the earth, after their kinds, went forth out of the ark.

17 The deluge covered the earth for 40 days. 18 The waters swelled and rose high on the earth, and the barge floated on the surface of the waters; 19 the waters swelled mightily on the earth, 20 till every high mountain under heaven was covered—the waters swelling 22 feet higher, till the mountains were covered,

8:13
    And it came to pass that in the 601
year of Noah's life: in the 1st month,
on the 1st day of that month: that the
waters were dried up from off the land,
and Noah removed the covering of the
ark, and looked, and behold, the face
of the Earth was dry.

8:14
    And in the 2nd month, on the 27th
day of that month, was the land dried.

8:15
    And Yahveh said unto Noah,

8:16
    "Come thou out of the ark,
you and your wife, and your sons
and their wives.

8:17
    Bring with you every living
creature, that they may be fruitful and
multiply abundantly in this part of the
world."

8:18
    So Noah and his family came out of
the ark.

8:19
    And every beast, every fowl, and
every moving creature that creeps upon
the Earth, came out of the ark in
families.

NOTE:
All the days and dates mentioned are Sabbaths except v.8:5

NOTE:
One SOLAR YEAR has passed since the flood started in 7:11.

Also it's good to know that all PROPHECIES pertaining to Yahveh's children are given in SOLAR days. All PROPHECIES pertaining to Satan and his evil works are given in months or moons.

NOTE:
Many of the animals already had multiplied in the ark.

20 And Noah built an altar unto the Lord; and took of every clean beast, and every clean fowl, and offered burnt offerings on the altar. 21 And the Lord smelled a sweet savour; and the Lord said in his heart, I will not again curse the ground any more for man's sake; for the imagination of man's heart is evil from his youth; neither will I again smite any more every thing living, as I have done. 22 While the earth remaineth, seedtime and harvest, and cold and heat, and summer and winter, and day and night shall not cease. 9:1 And God blessed Noah and his sons, and said unto them, Be fruitful, and multiply, and replenish the earth.

20 Then Noah built an altar to the Lord, and took of every clean animal and of every clean bird, and offered burnt offerings on the altar. 21 And when the Lord smelled the pleasing odor, the Lord said in his heart, "I will never again curse the ground because of man, for the imagination of man's heart is evil from his youth; neither will I ever again destroy every living creature as I have done. 22 While the earth remains, seedtime and harvest, cold and heat, summer and winter, day and night, shall not cease." 9:1 And God blessed Noah and his sons, and said to them, "Be fruitful and multiply, and fill the earth.

20 Then Noah built an altar to the Lord and, taking of every clean animal and of every clean bird, he offered burnt offerings on the altar. 21 The Lord smelled the pleasing odor, and the Lord said to Himself: "Never again will I doom the earth because of man, since the devisings of man's mind are evil from his youth; nor will I ever again destroy every living being, as I have done. 22 So long as the earth endures, seedtime and harvest, cold and heat, summer and winter, day and night, shall not cease." 9:1 God blessed Noah and his sons, and said to them, "Be fertile and increase, and fill the earth.

20 Then Noah built an altar to the Lord; ant took of every clean animal and of every clean fowl, and offered burnt offerings on the altar. 21 And the Lord smelled the sweet savour; and the Lord said in his heart, I will not again curse the ground any more for man's sake; for the inclination of man's heart is evil from his youth; neither will I again destroy any more every living thing, as I have done. 22 From henceforth, while the earth remains, seedtime and harvest, and cold and heat, and summer and winter, and day and night shall not cease. 9:1 And God blessed Noah and his sons, and said to them, Be fruitful, and multiply, and replenish the earth.

21 and every living creature perished, bird, beast, and animal, every reptile that crawls on earth, and every man. 22 Everything with the breath of life in its nostrils, whatever was on the dry land, died. 23 the Eternal blotted every living creature off the earth, men, beasts, reptiles, and birds; they were blotted off the earth, till only Noah and his company inside the barge were left. 24 For 150 days the waters swelled over the earth. 8:1 But God remembered Noah and all the living creatures and the animals that were with him in the barge; 2 God made a wind blow over the earth, till the sluices of heaven were closed; 3 and at the end of the 150 days, the waters began to subside. 4 In the seventh month, on the seventeenth day of the month, the barge grounded on the mountains of Armenia. 5 Till the tenth month the waters steadily subsided, and on the first day of the tenth month the tops of the mountains were seen; 6 Then Noah opened the window he had made in the barge, 7 and sent out a raven, which went flying here and there till the waters had dried off the earth. 8 He waited seven days and then sent out a dove, to see if the waters had drained off the earth;

8:20
    And Noah built an alter unto the
                    v.7:2
Lord and took of every **CLEAN BEAST** and

of every **CLEAN FOWL**, and offered them

up to the Lord.

8:21
    And Yahveh delighted in the savored

smell, and the Lord said in his heart,

"I will not again curse the **GROUND** for

man's sake, although the imagination

of his mind is evil from his youth.

Neither will I again destroy every

living thing, as I have done in the

FIRST WORLD AGE.

8:22
    As long as the Earth remains,

seedtime and harvest, hot and cold,

winter and summer, day and night shall

not cease."

CHAPTER NINE
9:1
    And Yahveh blessed Noah and his sons,

and said unto them,"Be fruitful, and

multiply, and repopulate this part of

the Earth.

NOTE:
This is the 1st
alter built.

NOTE:
Because of this
promise, there
will never be a
so called;
Nuclear Winter.

NOTE:
All people which
are of the
v.2:7
ADAMIC race,
come from the
generations of
Noah and or Cain.

2 And the fear of you and the dread of you shall be upon every beast of the earth, and upon every fowl of the air, upon all that moveth upon the earth, and upon all the fishes of the sea; into your hand are they delivered. 3 Every moving thing that liveth shall be meat for you; even as the green herb have I given you all things. 4 But flesh with the life thereof, which is the blood thereof, shall ye not eat.5 And surely your blood of your lives will I require; at the hand of every beast will I require it, and at the hand of man; at the hand of every man's brother will I require the life of man. 6 Whoso sheddeth man's blood, by man shall his blood be shed: for in the image of God made he man.

2 The fear of you and the dread of you shall be upon every beast of the earth, and upon every bird of the air, upon everything that creeps on the ground and all the fish in the sea; into your hand they are delivered. 3 Every moving thing that lives shall be food for you; and as I gave you the green plants, I give you everything. 4 Only you shall not eat flesh with its life, that is, its blood. 5 For your lifeblood I will surely require a reckoning; of every beast I will require it and of man; of every man's brother I will require the life of man. 6 Whoever sheds the blood of man, by man shall his blood be shed; for God made man in his own image.

2 The fear and the dread of you shall be upon all the beasts of the earth and upon all the birds of the sky—everything with which the earth is astir—and upon all the fish of the sea; they are given into your hand. 3 Every creature that lives shall be yours to eat; as with the green grasses, I give you all these. 4 You must not, however, eat flesh with its life-blood in it. 5 But for your own life-blood I will require a reckoning: I will require it of every beast; of man, too, will I require a reckoning for human life, of every man for that of his fellow man! 6 Whoever sheds the blood of man, By man shall his blood be shed; For in His image did God make man.

2 And the fear of you and the dread of you shall be upon every beast of the earth, and upon every fowl of the air, upon all that moves upon the earth, and all the fish of the sea; into your hand they are delivered. 3 Every moving thing that is alive shall be food for you; even as the green herb have I given you all things. 4 Only flesh with the life thereof, that is, the blood thereof, you shall not eat. 5 And surely your lifeblood will I avenge; of every beast will I avenge it, and at the hand of man; and at the hand of a man and his brother will I avenge the life of man. 6 Whoever sheds the blood of men, by men shall his blood be shed; for man was made in the image of God.

9 but, as the dove could find no rest for the sole of her foot, she flew back to him in the barge; he put his hand out, caught her and took her in beside him in the barge. 10 After waiting seven days more, he sent the dove out of the barge again; 11 in the evening the dove came back to him, and there, in her beak, was the fresh leaf of an olive! So Noah knew that the waters were drained off the earth.12 After waiting seven days more, he sent out the dove, but she never came back to him. 13 Then Noah removed the covering of the barge and looked out. There lay the surface of the ground, all dry! 14 on the 27th day of the second month, the earth itself was dry. 15 Then said God to Noah, 16 "Leave the barge, you and your wife and your sons and your sons' wives, 17 and take out every living thing that is with you, every creature, bird and beast and reptile, that they may swarm on earth and be fruitful and multiply on earth." 18 So Noah came out, along with his sons and his wife and his sons' wives; also every beast, every reptile, every fowl, everything that moves on earth, all came out of the barge, arranged in families.

9:2

And every beast of the Earth, and
every fowl of the air, and every fish
in the seas shall fear and dread you.
Into your hands are they delivered,
and   (mankind) **YOU**   shall be held responsible
for their preservation.

9:3

And along with the green herbs, I
give you **EVERY LIVING CREATURE FOR FOOD.**

9:4

But flesh with the   (blood) **LIFE**   still in
it, you shall not eat it.

9:5

And if you kill any beast; other
than for food and clothing, the blood
of you I will require and hold
responsible.

9:6

And if any man murders another man,
he shall be put to death, for in the
image of God was man made."

COMMENT:
CAPITAL PUNISHMENT

If you read Duet. 19:4-13, Yahveh tells us what we are to do if a man

is killed by another man. Verses 4-10 talks about an accidental death.

But verses 11-13 speak about what should happen to someone who MURDERS

another.

If a person is definitely guilty of MURDER, the punishment; told to

us by Yahveh, is to put the murderer to death. Some people say, "If we

put to death the murderer,than we ourselves are disobeying the Commandment;

Thou shall not kill.(Duet.5:17)" NOT SO, because the word kill should

really be translated MURDER. Thou shall not MURDER is the Commandment.

When we execute a murderer, it is the punishment for his crime, and so

it is not murder, it's justice.

Another argument is that some say: "Yahshua changed the Commandments."

These people, with their Bible in hand, will protest the executions outside

of the building where the punishments are carried out. Well they should

open their Bibles to Matt. 5:17-21.

> (change)
> Matt. 5:17   Think not that I have come to DESTROY THE LAW,
> (change)
> or the prophets. I am not come to DESTROY, but
>
> to fulfill. [Yahshua came to fulfill Prophecy,
> not to change the laws of the Bible.]

> Matt. 5:21   Ye have heard that it was said by them of old time,
> (murder)   (murder)
> Thou shall not KILL, and whosoever shall KILL
> (punishment)
> shall be in danger of the   JUDGMENT.

> It is approved by Yahveh, and our right, to execute a murderer.
> And as for the people who protest, they should read Duet.19:13.

> [the murderer]
> Duet. 19:13   Thine eye SHALL NOT PITY HIM, but thou shall
> (blotout/destroy) (the one guilty of murder.)
> PUT AWAY   THE GUILT OF INNOCENT BLOOD
> (your people)
> FROM ISREAL, that it may go well with thee.

> [Meaning, the family and friends of the one murdered
> will feel JUSTICE has been served.]

73

I would also like to mention the verses of Matt. 5:39 and Luke 6:29, which are about the turning of the other cheek, and loving your enemy. The word enemy is wrongly defined when speaking about these verses. The enemy mentioned are not so called thieves, muggers, murderers, or the people your country might be at war with. When Yahshua said,"Love your enemy,"He wasn't talking about the type of people mentioned above. The enemy Yahshua was talking about was any person who didn't believe in the true God: YAHVEH.

To Yahveh's people, all unbelievers, infidels, pagan worshipers, and so on, are considered, the enemy. Even if a man was unselfish, very generous, honorable,and so on, but maybe prayéd to a false god, he was considered; in a sense, the enemy.

If a poor person who worshiped a pagan god asked for your coat, Yahshua said,"Give it to him." Why? So that you could be an example of the type of person who worshiped Yahveh. But, if a robber came up to you and said,"Give me your coat," he is a criminal, and should be treated as one.

Also, the turning of the other cheek, is not a literal slap in the face. It is when you might be teaching the word of God, and they yell and swear and use ruff words against you.

Sometimes they do get violent. If they do, use your common sense and get out of there. But, if your walking down the street and some bully; for no reason, smacks you in the face, don't turn the other cheek and let him hit that one too. Smack him back and protect yourself. Or if an intruder brakes into your house, don't just stand there, grab a weapon and defend what is yours. These extremes and circumstances are approved by Yahveh and considered a righteous thing to do. Don't let Satan's followers have their way with you. Take a stand against crime, and Yahveh will bless you for it.

7 And you, be ye fruitful, and multiply; bring forth abundantly in the earth, and multiply therein. 8 And God spake unto Noah, and to his sons with him, saying, 9 And I, behold, I establish my covenant with you, and with your seed after you; 10 And with every living creature that is with you, of the fowl, of the cattle, and of every beast of the earth with you; from all that go out of the ark, to every beast of the earth. 11 And I will establish my covenant with you; neither shall all flesh be cut off any more by the waters of a flood; neither shall there any more be a flood to destroy the earth. 12 And God said, This is the token of the covenant which I make between me and you and every living creature that is with you, for perpetual generations: 13 I do set my bow in the cloud, and it shall be for a token of a covenant between me and the earth.

7 And you, be fruitful and multiply, bring forth abundantly on the earth and multiply in it." 8 Then God said to Noah and to his sons with him, "Behold, I establish my covenant with you and your descendants after you, 10 and with every living creature that is with you, the birds, the cattle, and every beast of the earth with you, as many as came out of the ark. 11 I establish my covenant with you, that never again shall all flesh be cut off by the waters of a flood, and never again shall there be a flood to destroy the earth." 12 And God said, "This is the sign of the covenant which I make between me and you and every living creature that is with you, for all future generations: 13 I set my bow in the cloud, and it shall be a sign of the covenant between me and the earth.

7 Be fertile, then, and increase; abound on the earth and increase on it," 8 And God said to Noah and to his sons with him, 9 "I now establish My covenant with you and your offspring to come, 10 and with every living thing that is with you—birds, cattle, and every wild beast as well—all that have come out of the ark, every living thing on earth. 11 I will maintain My covenant with you: never again shall all flesh be cut off by the waters of a flood, and never again shall there be a flood to destroy the earth." 12 God further said, "This is the sign that I set for the covenant between Me and you, and every living creature with you, for all ages to come. 13 I have set My bow in the clouds, and it shall serve as a sign of the covenant between Me and the earth.

7 As for you, be fruitful, and multiply; bring forth abundantly on the earth, and multiply in it. 8 And God spoke to Noah, and to his sons with him, saying, 9 As for me, behold, I will establish my covenant with you and with your descendants after you; 10 And with every living creature that is with you, the fowl, the cattle, and every wild beast of the earth with you; with all that come out of the ark, and with every beast of the earth. 11 And I will establish my covenant with you; so that never again shall all flesh perish by the waters of a flood; neither shall there any more be a flood to destroy the earth. 12 And God said to Noah, This is the sign of the covenant which I make between Me and you and every living creature that is with you, for perpetual generations: 13 I set my bow in the clouds, and it shall be a sign of a covenant between Me and the earth.

20 Then Noah built an altar to the Eternal; he took some clean beasts and birds of every kind and burned them in sacrifice on the altar, and when the Eternal smelt the soothing fragrance, the Eternal said to himself, "Never again will I curse the ground, though the bent of man's mind is indeed towards evil from his youth; never again will I destroy every living creature as I have done. 22 So long as earth remains, seedtime and harvest, cold and heat, summer and winter, day and night, shall never cease." 9:1 And God blessed Noah and his sons, bidding them, "Be fruitful and multiply and replenish the earth.

9:7
   "And you be fruitful and multiply
abundantly in the Earth."

9:8
   And Yahveh spoke unto Noah and his
sons saying,

9:9
   "I will establish my covenant with you
and with all the generations after you.

9:10
   And with every living creature that
is with you, and is of the Earth, I also
establish my covenant.

9:11
   I will never again; with a flood of
water, destroy all flesh, and I will
never again destroy the Heavens and the
Earth with water, as I did in

THE FIRST WORLD AGE."

9:12
   And Yahveh said,"This sign of the
covenant which I make between Me and you,
and every living creature of the Earth,
                        (forever)
shall be for   **PERPETUAL GENERATIONS.**

9:13
   I do set My rainbow in the clouds
and it shall be the sign of the promise
which is between Me and the Earth.

14 And it shall come to pass, when I bring a cloud over the earth, that the bow shall be seen in the cloud: 15 And I will remember my covenant, which is between me and you and every living creature of all flesh; and the waters shall no more become a flood to destroy all flesh. 16 And the bow shall be in the cloud; and I will look upon it, that I may remember the everlasting covenant between God and every living creature of all flesh that is upon the earth. 17 And God said unto Noah, This is the token of the covenant, which I have established between me and all flesh that is upon the earth. 18 And the sons of Noah, that went forth of the ark, were Shem, and Ham, and Japheth: and Ham is the father of Canaan.

RSV

14 When I bring clouds over the earth and the bow is seen in the clouds, 15 I will remember my covenant which is between me and you and every living creature of all flesh; and the waters shall never again become a flood to destroy all flesh. 16 When the bow is in the clouds, I will look upon it and remember the everlasting covenant between God and every living creature of all flesh that is upon the earth." 17 God said to Noah, "This is the sign of the covenant which I have established between me and all flesh that is upon the earth." 18 The sons of Noah who went forth from the ark were Shem, Ham, and Japheth. Ham was the father of Canaan.

TANAKH

14 When I bring clouds over the earth, and the bow appears in the clouds, 15 I will remember My covenant between Me and you and every living creature among all flesh, so that the waters shall never again become a flood to destroy all flesh. 16 When the bow is in the clouds, I will see it and remember the everlasting covenant between God and all living creatures, all flesh that is on earth. 17 That," God said to Noah, "shall be the sign of the covenant that I have established between Me and all flesh that is on earth." 18 The sons of Noah who came out of the ark were Shem, Ham, and Japheth—Ham being the father of Canaan.

HOLY BIBLE GNL

14 And it shall come to pass, when I bring clouds over the earth, that the bow shall be seen in the clouds; 15 And I will remember my covenant, which is between me and you and every living creature that is with you of all flesh; and the waters shall no more become a flood to destroy all flesh. 16 And the bow shall be in the clouds; and I will look upon it as a remembrance of the everlasting covenant between God and every living creature of all flesh that is upon the earth. 17 And God said to Noah, This is the sign of the covenant which I have established between me and all the flesh that is upon the earth. 18 The sons of Noah who went out forth out of the ark were Shem and Ham and Japheth; and Ham is the father of Canaan.

HOLY BIBLE JM

2 The dread of you and terror of you shall be on every beast of the earth and every bird of the air; for they are now in your power, with every reptile of the land and every fish within the sea. 3 Every moving thing that is alive is to be food for you; I give you them all, as once I gave you the green growth. 4 Only, you must never eat flesh with the life (that is, the blood) in it. 5 And I will avenge the shedding of your own life-blood; I will avenge it on any beast, I will avenge man's life on man, upon his brotherman; 6 whoever sheds human blood, by human hands shall his own blood be shed—for God made man in his own likeness. 7 As for you, be fruitful and multiply; breed freely on earth and subdue it." 8 Then said God to Noah and also to his sons, "I now ratify my compact with you and your descendants, 10 and with every living creature in your company, with any bird or beast or animal whatsoever that leaves the barge, with every beast of the earth:

9:14

And it shall come to pass, that when I bring a cloud over the Earth, that a rainbow shall be seen.

9:15

And I will remember my covenant which is between Me and you and every living creature of the Earth. And the waters shall never again become a flood to destroy all flesh.

9:16

And the rainbow shall be in the cloud; and I **WILL LOOK** upon it; [Yahveh is always watching over us.] that I may remember the everlasting covenant."

9:17

And Yahveh said unto Noah, "The rainbow is the sign of the promise, established between Me and all flesh upon the Earth.

9:18

And the sons of Noah that went forth of the ark were, Shem, Ham, and Japheth: and **Ham** is the **FATHER OF CANAAN.** [Canaan was not yet born at this time.]

NOTE:
There are many promises made by Yahveh to his (elect) PEOPLE. A good example of the word elect, is in Matt. 24:22-24.

Isaiah 54:9 (the elect are) FOR THIS IS as the waters of Noah unto me: for as I have sworn that the waters of Noah should no more go over the Earth: so have I sworn that I would not be (angry) WROTH with thee, nor rebuke thee.

Isaiah 54:10 For the mountains shall depart, and the hills be removed, but my kindness shall not depart from thee, neither shall the covenant of my peace be removed, saith the Lord that hath mercy on thee.

19 These are the three sons of Noah: and of them was the whole earth overspread. 20 And Noah began to be an husbandman, and he planted a vineyard: 21 And he drank of the wine, and was drunken; and he was uncovered within his tent. 22 And Ham, the father of Canaan, saw the nakedness of his father, and told his two brethren without. 23 And Shem and Japheth took a garment, and laid it upon both their shoulders, and went backward, and covered the nakedness of their father; and their faces were backward, and they saw not their father's nakedness. 24 And Noah awoke from his wine, and knew what his younger son had done unto him.

19 These three were the sons of Noah; and from these the whole earth was peopled. 20 Noah was the first tiller of the soil. He planted a vineyard; 21 and he drank of the wine, and became drunk, and lay uncovered in his tent. 22 And Ham, the father of Canaan, saw the nakedness of his father, and told his two brothers outside. 23 Then Shem and Japheth took a garment, laid it upon their shoulders, and walked backward and covered the nakedness of their father; their faces were turned away, and they did not see their father's nakedness. 24 When Noah awoke from his wine and knew what his youngest son had done to him,

19 These three were the sons of Noah, and from these the whole world branched out. 20 Noah, the till of the soil, was the first to plant a vineyard. 21 He drank of the wine and became drunk, and he uncovered himself within his tent. 22 Ham, the father of Canaan, saw his father's nakedness and told his two brothers outside. 23 But Shem and Japheth took a cloth, placed it against both their backs and, walking backward, they covered their father's nakedness; their faces were turned the other way, so that they did not see their father's nakedness. 24 When Noah woke up from his wine and learned what his youngest son had done to him,

19 These three were the sons of Noah; and from them the people spread throughout the earth. 20 And Noah began to till the ground; and he planed a vineyard; 21 And he drank of its wine, and became drunken; and he was uncovered within his tent. 22 And Ham, the father of Canaan, saw the nakedness of his father, and he told his two brothers outside. 23 And Shem and Japheth took a mantle and laid it upon both their shoulders and walked backward and covered the nakedness of their father; and their faces were backward and they did not see their father's nakedness. 24 When Noah awoke from his wine and knew what his younger son had done to him,

11 I ratify my compact with you, that never again shall all living creatures be swept away by the waters of the deluge, that never again shall there be a deluge to destroy the earth. 12 Here," said God, "is the symbol of the compact that I make with you and all the living creatures in your company for endless generations: 13 in the clouds I set my rainbow, as a symbol of the compact between myself and the earth. 14 whenever I cloud over the earth, once the rainbow appears in the clouds, 15 then I will remember my compact with you and every living creature whatsoever, and the waters shall never again become a deluge to destroy every creature. 16 When the rainbow appears in the clouds, I will look at it to remind me of the lasting compact between God and every living creature whatsoever upon earth. 17 This," God said to Noah, "is the symbol of the compact that I ratify between myself and every creature upon earth." 18 The sons of Noah who came out of the barge were Shem, Ham, and Japheth [[Ham was the father of Canaan]]. 19 These three were the sons of Noah, and from them people spread all over the earth. 20 Noah the farmer was the first to plant a vineyard; 21 he drank some of the wine and, becoming drunk, lay uncovered inside his tent.

9:19
These are the three sons of Noah,
and of them, was the whole Earth
v.2:7
repopulated with the **ADAMITE RACE.**

[The sons of Cain also contribute

to this growth.]

9:20   (Farmer)
And Noah was a **MAN OF THE GROUND**

and he planted a vineyard.

9:21
And Noah drank of the wine and was

drunken; and he was uncovered within

his tent.

9:22
And Ham, **THE FATHER OF CANAAN,** saw

THE NAKEDNESS OF HIS FATHER, and told

his two brothers outside.

9:23
And Shem and Japheth took a garment

and laid it upon both their shoulders

and went in backward, and covered
(Noah's wife)
THE NAKEDNESS OF THEIR FATHER, and

their faces were backward, and they saw

not their father's nakedness.

9:24
And Noah sobered up from his wine,

and he knew what his son, Ham had done.

NOTE:
THE NAKEDNESS OF
HIS FATHER.
Lev. 18:8
(nude body)
The NAKEDNESS of thy
father's wife shall
thou not uncover:
IT IS THY FATHER'S
NAKEDNESS.

Lev. 20:11
(Ham)
And the MAN that
4904
7901
LIETH with his
father's wife hath
uncovered HIS
FATHER'S NAKEDNESS:

1) 4904
mishkab

2) 7901
shakab

Both meaning to
sleep with, or to
lie with, to have
sex.

COMMENT:
Ham had sexual
intercourse with
(Noah's wife)
HIS MOTHER,
thus becoming the
FATHER OF CANAAN.

25 And he said, Cursed be Canaan; a servant of servants shall he be unto his brethren. 26 And he said, Blessed be the Lord God of Shem; and Canaan shall be his servant. 27 God shall enlarge Japheth, and he shall dwell in the tents of Shem; and Canaan shall be his servant. 28 And Noah lived after the flood 350 years. 29 And all the days of Noah were 950 years: and he died.

25 he said, "Cursed be Canaan; a slave of slaves shall he be to his brothers." 26 He also said, "Blessed by the Lord my God be Shem; and let Canaan be his slave. 27 God enlarge Japheth, and let him dwell in the tents of Shem; and let Canaan be his slave." 28 After the flood Noah lived 350 years. 29 All the days of Noah were 950 years; and he died.

25 he said, "Cursed be Canaan; the lowest of slaves shall he be to his brothers." 26 And he said, "Blessed be the Lord. the God of Shem; let Canaan be a slave to them. 27 May God enlarge Japheth, And let him dwell in the tents of Shem; And let Canaan be a slave to them." 28 Noah lived after the flood 350 years. 29 And all the days of Noah came to be 950 years; then he died.

25 He said, Cursed be Canaan; a servant of servants shall he be to his brothers. 26 Then he said, Blessed be the Lord God of Shem; and let Canaan be his servant. 27 God shall enrich Japheth, and he shall dwell in the tents of Shem; and Canaan shall be their servant. 28 And Noah lived after the flood 350 years. 29 And all the days of Noah were 950 years, and he died.

22 When [[Ham the father of]] Canaan saw his father naked, he told his two brothers outside; 23 And Shem and Japheth took a mantle and laid it upon both their shoulders and walked backward and covered the nakedness of their father; and their faces were backward and they did not see their father's nakedness. 24 When Noah awoke from his wine and knew what his younger son had done to him, 25 He said, Cursed be Canaan; a servant of servants shall he be to his brothers. 26 Then he said, Blessed be the Lord God of Shem; and let Canaan be his servant. 27 May God enlarge Japheth! May he be welcome in the tents of Shem, and have Canaan as his slave!" 28 After the deluge Noah lived 350 years. 29 Thus Noah lived for 950 years in all; and then he died.

9:25
And Noah said,"Cursed be Canaan, a
servant of servants shall he be unto his
brethren."

9:26
And he said,"Blessed be Yahveh,
God of Shem: Canaan shall be his servant.

9:27
And as the result of what Ham has
done, Yahveh shall enlarge Japheth, and
(tents)
Yahveh shall dwell in the **TABERNACLES**
of Shem, and Canaan shall be his servant.

9:28
And Noah lived after the flood
350 years.

9:29
And all the days of Noah were 950
years and he died.

THE WHOLE PICTURE

PART ONE: In The Beginning GOD.

In this chapter, we're going to recapture for your mind the truths and information that was contained in the first ten chapters of Genesis. I know it's hard to read a book when it tells you to look up Scriptures as it did for the studies, but I did my best to keep them short and straight to the point. I wanted to keep **GENESIS: A CLOSER LOOK** more in the Biblical style. Secondly, by putting in the **SCRIPTURE SEARCH**, it would get you to dig into your own Bibles while proving to yourself the truths and information contained.

I do hope you did the searches, because in this recap, I am only going to refer the specific version of the Scripture the information comes from. I will write some scriptures, but for the most part, I will use only the basics of them.

We'll start **THE WHOLE PICTURE** from the very beginning. There was nothing in existence, no dust, molecules, not even an atom. **YAHVEH** was the only **BEING** in existence. Before anything else, **GOD WAS.** *Rev. 1:8, I am Alpha and Omega, the beginning and the ending. Isaiah 41:4 I the Lord, the first, and with the last; I am He.* Yahveh has always been in existence. But what and who is God? Well in *John 4:24* it says, *God is Spirit,* well what is Spirit? *John 3:8* it says, *Spirit moves, and is like the wind. Acts 2:17 I will pour out my Spirit.* So it's also like water. *Col. 1:15 Who is the image of the invisible God.* So Spirit is also invisible. And in *II Cor. 4:18 for the things which are seen are temporal; but the things which are not seen are eternal,* meaning they don't age, die, etc. So to conclude, Spirit is is like invisible water, which is as light as air, and moves like the wind, and will never corrupt or die.

Now let's see who Yahveh is. We know He was before every-thing. *John 17:5 before the world was. Psalm 90:2 from ever-lasting to everlasting, there was God.* And in *Heb. 7:3 Without father, without mother, without* **DESCENT**, *(genealogy) having neither begin-ning of days, nor end of life;. Prov. 8:1-30 God is wisdom. I Sam 2:3 God is knowledge. Psalms 3:3 He is a shield and an uplifter. Ps. 5:8 He leads us. Ps. 9:9 He is our refuse.* Yahveh is many things to us, but most of all, He loves and cares about everyone of us. Now let's continue.

John 1:1-4 In the beginning was the **WORD**, *and the* **WORD** *was with God, and the* **WORD** *was God. 2) The same was in the beginning with God. 3) All things were made by Him; and without Him was not any thing made that was made.* Now I'm going out on a limb with this belief and explanation, but it's what I feel is truth.

If you read on to *John 1:14* it says, *And the* **WORD** *was made flesh, and dwelt among us, (and we behold his glory. The glory as of the only begotten of the father,) full of grace and truth.* Now we all know that the **WORD** that was made flesh is Jesus. [Yahshua]

How could this be? The **WORD** was with God, the **WORD** was God, and the **WORD** was made flesh. [Yahshua] Well let's start by asking the question, what is a word?

A word is what comes out of a person's mouth; in voice form, when speaking. In this sense, both voice and words are the same. In *Gen. 1:3* God said **LET THERE BE LIGHT**, *and there became light.* Now, who made the light come into existence?

Who really made the light? *John 1:3, All things were made by Him; [the word] and without him was not any thing made that was made.* Yahveh says the **WORD** made the light.

This could only lead to one conclusion, Yahveh being the very unselfish spirit He is, gave all the credit to his **VOICE**. He could of said, I made the light, or I did it all, but no Yahveh gave His voice all the credit. He gave His voice, **PERSONAL EXISTENCE**.

Even ourselves do this at times. There's the saying; MY EYES DECEIVED ME. Here we are putting the blame on our eyes, instead of ourselves, or MY KNEE GAVE OUT. There are many times in our life that we give parts of our bodies; **PERSONAL EXISTENCE**. And this is what I truly believe Yahveh did.

And here's one more Scripture for proof, *Psalm 33:6 by the* (voice) (angels) *WORD of the Lord were the Heavens made; and all the HOST* (Yahveh's) *of them by the BREATH of HIS mouth.*

OK, if that wasn't enough, this next step is going to be even tougher, especially for the Christian community. **AND THE WORD WAS MADE FLESH**. If the **WORD** was Yahveh's voice, then we must also believe it was Yahveh himself that was made flesh.

To most of us, we like referring to God as Father. If the **WORD** is Yahveh himself, why would we call Him **THE SON OF GOD?** To explain this better, let's look at it from a business point of view. In a company, you have a President and then next in line you have a vice-president, after that you have the employees.

In *I Cor. 11:3* we have a similar set up. It says, *But I would have you know, that the head of every man is Christ; and the head of the woman is the man; and the head of Christ is God.*

Here we have a business type set up. Yahveh is the President, Yahshua is the vice-president, and we are the employees.

85

Now in some small companies the President is also the vice-president. One person occupies both offices. In *John 14:8 Philip saith unto Him, Lord, shew us the Father, and it* sufficeth *us.* (will satisfy) *9) Jesus saith unto him, Have I been so long time with you, and yet hast thou not known me, Philip?* **HE THAT HATH SEEN ME HATH SEEN THE FATHER**: *and how sayest thou then, Shew us the Father?*

It is perfectly clear that Yahveh holds both offices. He is the Father, and He is the Son. It would be impossible for you to see the Father and the Son in the same room. To make it a little more understandable, I'm going to use an old TV show as an example.

The show is, "The Patty Duke Show." It's about two identical cousins, both characters were played by the same actress, Patty Duke.

Just as it was impossible to see both cousins at the same time, [in reality] so it is with the Father and the Son. Both offices, the Father and the Son, are played by Yahveh. As a matter of fact, there is yet another role in which Yahveh played.

If you remember, we read in *Heb. 7:3 Without father, without mother, without* **DESCENT**, *having neither beginning of days,* (genealogy) *nor end of life;* **BUT MADE LIKE UNTO** *the Son of God;* abideth (Yahshua) (remaining) *a priest continually.* We all know that this Scripture is talking about Yahshua right? **WRONG!**

Even though we know now that Yahveh and Yahshua are the same person, and that He had no father or mother, this Scripture, however, is talking about **MELCHISEDEC**, king of Salem, **PRIEST OF THE MOST HIGH GOD**.

Start at the beginning of the chapter, it's perfectly clear that these Scriptures are talking about **MELCHISEDEC**. If He had no father, no mother, no descent, it's obvious that **MELCHISEDEC** was God also.

That is why I highlighted in verse three; "but made like unto the Son of God."

So again we find Yahveh becoming flesh and blood and playing yet another role here on Earth, but with a different name. Melchisedec was truly God in the flesh.

Even though Yahveh held both offices, Melchisedec's role was not as important as Yahshua's. When He died on **THE CROSS** for us, it showed just how much the Father loves us. Yahshua, the **VOICE** and the **WORD OF GOD** will always be the only way to the Father.

As it reads in *John 14:6 **I AM THE WAY, THE TRUTH, AND THE LIFE: NO MAN COMETH UNTO THE FATHER, BUT BY ME.***

I know many of you will think this view of God is off the wall, but it's where my years of studying the Bible have brought me. Even though we may differ in our beliefs of God, there is one Scripture we can all agree on, and that one is found in *I John 4:16 **GOD IS LOVE** and he that dwelleth in love dwelleth in God, and God in him.*

PART TWO: CREATED, the HEAVENS and the EARTH

The first of Yahveh's creations were the **ANGELS**. The word, Angel, if you look it up in your Strong's Concordance, means **MESSENGER**. They are not ghosts with wings.

Whenever the word Angel is mentioned in the Bible, it means God's messenger. And from now on, I will use the word **SPIRIT BEING**, as to **HUMAN BEING**, which is the same thing, only in flesh and blood body.

In *Jer. 33:22* it says, *as the* **HOST** (spirit beings) *of heaven cannot be numbered, neither the sand of the sea measured: in Psalm 68:17 the chariots of God are twenty thousand, even thousands of* **ANGELS** (spirit beings):

It's safe to say that Yahveh created millions upon millions of Spirit Beings. Many times they are called, **SONS OF GOD**. [Gen. 6:2 Job 1:6 2:1] And in Chapter 38 of Job, while Yahveh was creating the Heavens and the Earth, it says that *the* **MORNING STARS** (future Fallen Angels) *sang together, and the* **SONS OF GOD** (Elect) *shouted for joy.*

This is why I believe the **ANGELS** (spirit beings) were Yahveh's first creations. They were already there when He started created all things.

In this chapter, Yahveh is putting Job in his place. You could say Yahveh is putting all of mankind in it's place, because most of man's knowledge is foolishness unto Him.

Verse 4 asked, *Where were you when I [Yahveh] laid the foundations of the Earth?* Verse 5, *Who made all the stars?* Verse 6, *What keeps the Earth in one place?*

In this whole chapter, Yahveh is asking man if he knows how He created and keeps in control the Universe and all the life within it. There's only one answer, **WE DON'T KNOW**.

Let's move to another part of God's word which has more information on this subject. Proverbs chapter eight.

In this chapter, **WISDOM** is talking to mankind. Verse 4 says, *Unto you, O men, I call; and my voice is to the* **SONS OF MAN**.
(you)
(naive)
5) O ye **SIMPLE**, *understand wisdom: and, ye fools, be ye of an understanding heart. 6) Hear; for I will speak of excellent things; and the opening of my lips shall be right things. 7) For my mouth shall speak truth; and wickedness is an abomination to my lips. 8) All the words of my mouth are in righteousness; there is nothing froward or perverse in them. 9) They are all plain to him that understandeth, and right to them that find knowledge. 10) Receive my instruction, and not silver; and knowledge rather than choice gold. 11) For wisdom is better than rubies; and all the things that may be desired are not to be compared to it. 12) I wisdom dwell with prudence, and find out knowledge of witty inventions.*
(To revere)
13) **THE FEAR OF** *the Lord is to hate evil: pride, and arrogancy, and the evil way, and the froward mouth, do I hate. 14) Counsel is mine, and sound wisdom: I am understanding; I have strength. 15) By me kings reign, and princes decree justice. 16) By me princess rule, and nobles, even all the judges of the earth. 17) I love them that love me; and those* **THAT SEEK ME** *early shall find me. 18) Riches and honour are with me; yea, durable riches and righteousness. 19) My* **FRUIT** *is better than gold, yea, than fine gold; and my revenue than choice silver. 20) I lead in the way of righteousness, in the midst of the paths of judgment: 21) That I may cause those that love me to inherit substance; and I will fill their treasures. 22) The Lord possessed me [wisdom] in the beginning of his way, before His* **WORKS OF OLD**. *23) I was set up*

from everlasting, from the beginning, (before) *or ever the Earth was. 24)* (oceans) *When there were no depths, I was brought forth; when there were no fountains abounding with water. 25) Before the mountains were settled, before the hills was I brought forth: 26) While as yet He had not made the Earth, nor the fields, nor the highest part of the dust of the world.* [atoms] *27) When He prepared the Heavens, I was there: when He set a compass upon the face of the depth: 28) When He established the clouds above: when He strengthened the fountains of the deep: 29) When He gave to the sea His decree, that the waters should not pass His commandment: when He appointed the foundations of the Earth: 30) Then I was by Him, as one brought up with Him: and I was daily His delight, rejoicing always before Him; 31) Rejoicing in the habitable part of **HIS EARTH**; and my delights were with the sons of men. 32) Now therefore hearken unto me, O ye children: for blessed are they that keep my ways. 33) Hear instruction, and be wise, and refuse it not. 34) Blessed is the man that heareth me, watching daily at my gates, waiting at the posts of my doors. 35) For whoso findeth me findeth life,* (eternal) *and shall obtain favour of the Lord. 36) But he that sinneth against me wrongeth his own* (body) ***SOUL:** all they that hate me love death.*

When you seek wisdom, you seek the Lord. And in *Psalms* 111:10 it says, (to revere) **THE FEAR OF** *the Lord is the beginning of wisdom: a good understanding have all they that do His commandments: His praise endureth for ever.*

We should always seek the wisdom of the Lord diligently. Yahveh will never lead us down the wrong path.

Now to continue forward, lets go back (ha, ha) to verse 22.

It says, *The Lord possessed me* [wisdom] *in the beginning of His way, before His WORKS OF OLD.* Well, what were Yahveh's **WORKS OF OLD**? To find this, we must turn to II Peter chapter three.

In verse 5 it reads, *For this they willingly are ignorant of, that by the WORD of God the Heavens WERE OF OLD, and the*
(emerging)
Earth standing out of the water and in the water: 6) Whereby the WORLD THAT THEN WAS, being overflowed with water, PERISHED: 7) But the Heavens and the Earth, WHICH ARE
(for)
NOW, by the same WORD are kept in store, reserved unto fire
(on)   (the destruction)
against the day of judgment and perdition of ungodly men.

In these three verses, we have **THE HEAVENS AND EARTH; THAT THEN WAS,** and we also have **THE HEAVENS AND EARTH; WHICH ARE NOW.** At times I will refer to these as **THE FIRST WORLD AGE,** and **THE SECOND WORLD AGE.**

The **FIRST WORLD AGE,** we are told in verse 6, being over-flowed with water, **PERISHED.** Now I know many of you reading this will say that this was the flood of Noah. This is not so. Let's turn back to *Genesis 1:1,2. In the beginning God created the Heavens and the Earth. 2) And the Earth* (became) *WAS without form, and void; and darkness was upon the face of the deep. And the spirit of God moved upon the face of the waters.* Now in verse 2 the word **WAS** is the Hebrew word hayah, (1961) which means, **TO BECOME.**

The Heavens and the Earth were not created void, and without form, they became void and without form, and to prove this knowl-edge to you let's turn to *Isaiah 45:18.* It reads, *For thus saith the Lord that created the Heavens; God himself that formed the Earth and made it; He hath established it, He created it NOT IN VAIN, he* (no one) *formed it to be INHABITED: I am the Lord; and there is none else.*

That word **VAIN** is the Hebrew word tohuw, (8414) which means confusion, empty place, without form, waste. It is the same word used in Gen. 1:2, translated **WITHOUT FORM**. Yahveh did not create the Heavens and the Earth void, and without form, they became that way. In *I. Cor. 14:33* it says, *For God is not the author of **CONFUSION**, but of peace.* Everything Yahveh creates is complete and perfect, not void and without form.

So the next question we have to ask is, WHAT HAPPENED AND HOW DID THE HEAVENS AND THE EARTH GET THIS WAY? Well to find the answer, let's start at Jer. 4:22. Here Yahveh is telling us about the destruction of the Heavens and Earth **THAT THEN WAS**, or as I put it, **THE FIRST WORLD AGE.**

22) For my people is foolish, (are stupid) *they have not known me; they are sottish children, and they have* (no) *none understanding: they are wise to do evil, but to do good they have no knowledge.*
23) I beheld (remember) *the Earth, and lo, it was **WITHOUT FORM**, and **VOID**; and **THE HEAVENS**, and **THEY HAD NO LIGHT**. 24) I beheld* (looked at) *the mountains, and lo, they trembled, and all the hills moved lightly. 25) I beheld,* (looked) *and, lo, **THERE WAS NO MAN**, and all the birds of the Heavens were* (dead) *fled. 26) I beheld, and lo, the fruitful place was a **WILDERNESS**, and all the **CITIES** thereof were broken down at the presence of the Lord, by his fierce anger. 27) For thus hath the Lord said, The whole land shall be desolate; yet I **WILL NOT MAKE A FULL END**. 28) For this shall the earth mourn, and the **HEAVENS ABOVE BE BLACK**: because I have spoken it, I have purposed it, and will not repent, neither will I turn back from it.*

This is definitely not Noah's flood. The reason I can say this is, in verse 23 the Heavens, they had no light. Verse 28 the Heavens above were made black, and in verse 25, **THERE WAS NO MAN**.

In Noah's flood, the heavens **WERE NOT** destroyed, and there were still men on the Earth. So, it's obvious that the destruction here is of the **FIRST WORLD AGE** and not the Great Deluge destruction which occurred in Noah's time. But why, and who was to blame for Yahveh to go to such extremes?

As you read earlier, the first of Yahveh's creations were the (spirit beings) **ANGELS**. So far there has been no mention of a **FLESH AND BLOOD,** human being.

There can be only one answer; the **WORLD THAT THEN WAS** or the **FIRST WORLD AGE** was inhabited by Yahveh's first creation, the Angels.

These **SPIRIT BEINGS** dwelt on the Earth just as we do today. If you go back to *Jer. 4:26* it says, *and all the CITIES thereof were broken down.* Here cities are mentioned, and where there are cities, there has to be buildings, and where there are buildings, there has to be a government. It may be hard to fathom, but the (spirit beings) **ANGELS** are no different then we ourselves; except, their essence dwells in a **SPIRIT BODY;** and our essence dwells in a **FLESH AND BLOOD** body.

Another difference is that we as Human Beings consist of two genders, male and female, whereas Spirit Beings have no gender.

Now, getting back to the First World Age, I mentioned a government. If you have cities, buildings, and millions upon millions of followers, it's safe to say that this is a kingdom. And

who could be more perfet to rule over this kingdom but Yahveh.
Creator and Father of us all.

It will never be a problem for me to have Yahveh my King
and my Father, and I hope you too can say the same.

AMEN.

PART THREE: But because of the REBELLION of LUCIFER.

As I mentioned at the end of Part two, the **FIRST WORLD AGE** consisted of Spirit Beings. Yahveh created the Earth for them to have a place to live.

They dwelled on this planet just as we do today. The Earth was home to them. I would also like to mention that the Earth back then was one huge land mass. It wasn't split apart as it is today with the different continents. We read this in *II Peter 3:5* (emerging) *and the Earth standing out of the water and in the water.*

Only after millions of years of moving about has the Earth spit up as it is today.

There is also no way of gauging exactly how old this Earth really is, but take it from me it's many millions of years old.

Now as I was saying, the Earth of the First World Age was inhabited by God's children, the Angels.

For more knowledge of this, let's turn to Ezek. 28. In this chapter, we can find out just what went wrong and why the First World Age was destroyed by Yahveh.

We're going to start at verse 12, which is before the destruc- (shout out) tion. It says, *Son of man, take up a lamentation upon the* (Lucifer) *king of Tyrus, and say to him, Thus saith the Lord God;*

Thou sealest up the sum, [you are the complete and finished pattern of all my children] *full of wisdom, and perfect in beauty.*

13) Thou hast been in Eden the **GARDEN OF GOD***; every precious stone was thy covering, the sardius, topaz, and the diamond, the beryl, the onyx, and the jasper, the sapphire, the emerald, and* (drums) *the carbuncle, and gold: the workmanship of thy tabrets and of thy pipes was prepared in thee in the day that thou wast* *created.* [created in him was the ability to play the most beautiful music]

14) **THOU ART THE ANOINTED CHERUB THAT**
(protected me)
COVERETH; *and I have set thee so: thou wast upon the holy mountain of God;* [heaven] *thou hast walked up and down in the midst of the stones of fire. 15) Thou wast perfect in thy ways*
(sin)
from the day that thou wast created, till iniquity was found in thee.

16) By the multitude of thy merchandise they have filled the midst of thee with violence, and thou hast sinned: therefore I will cast thee as profane out of the mountain of God: and I will destroy thee, O covering cherub, from the midst of the stones of
(mind)   (filled)
fire. 17) Thine heart was lifted up because of thy beauty, thou
(perfection)
hast corrupted thy wisdom by reason of thy brightness: I will lay thee before kings, that they may behold thee.

18) Thou hast defiled thy sanctuaries by the **MULTITUDE** *of*
(trade)
thine iniquities, by the iniquity of thy traffic; [a multitude of sins which Lucifer refused to repent of and ask Yahveh for forgiveness.] *therefore will I bring forth a* [consuming] *fire from the*
(turn)
midst of thee, it shall devour thee, and I will bring thee to ashes upon the Earth in the sight of all them that behold thee. 19) All they that know thee among the people shall be astonished at thee: thou shalt be a terror, and never shall thou be any more.

As we just read, Lucifer was the most beautiful Being Yahveh created. But after, who knows how much time, he became blind of who he really was.

Power, pride, and beauty corrupted his mind. At times, these Spirit Beings did sin, but like ourselves Yahveh forgave them when they repented.

Verse 18 says by the **MULTITUDE OF THINE INIQUITIES.** (sins)

Here we have a multitude of sins with no repentance or remorse. Lucifer was doing whatever he wanted to with no regard to Yahveh or the others. Having; what he thought, the same power and ability of Yahveh. Lucifer wanted to take over the throne of God.

These types of minds exist even today. All over the world there are leaders of countries and kingdoms who are trying to take control of other countries and kingdoms.

They are power hungry **TYRANTS**, and this is what Lucifer became within the Kingdom of God, and it is also why the First World Age was destroyed.

To get a better understanding let's go to *Isaiah 14:12*, it says, *How art thou fallen from Heaven, O Lucifer, son of the morning! how art thou cut down to the ground, which didst weaken the nations!*

13) For thou hast said in thine heart, (to himself) *I will ascend into heaven, I will exalt my throne above the* (sons) *stars of God: I will sit also upon the mount of the congregation,* (Zion) *in the sides of the north.* [Isaiah 48:2, II Thes. 2:4] *14) I will ascend above the heights of the clouds; I will be **LIKE** the Most High.*

15) Yet thou shalt be brought down to hell, to the sides of the pit. [Rev. 20:3] *16) They that see thee shall narrowly look upon thee, and consider thee, saying, **IS THIS THE MAN** that made the earth tremble, that did shake kingdoms; 17) that made **THE WORLD AS A WILDERNESS, AND DESTROYED THE CITIES THEREOF;*** [Jer.4:26] *that opened not the house of his prisoners?* (couldn't unlock) (God's)

Again we read that Lucifer was rebelling against God and trying to overthrow God's Kingdom. I would also like mention that in Verse 16 it says, is this the **MAN?**

Here we have a Spirit created Being, but Yahveh is calling him a man.

Like I said before, it makes no difference if one is composed of a spirit body or a flesh and blood body, we are all children of God.

Now let's go back to Ezekiel 28, starting this time in verse 2) *Son of man, say unto the prince of Tyrus, Thus saith the Lord God; because thine heart* (mind) *is lifted up, and thou hast said, I am a God, I sit in the seat of God, in the midst of the* (people) *seas; yet thou art* **A MAN**, *and not God, though thou set thine heart* (mind) *as the heart* (mind) *of God: 3) Behold, thou art wiser than Daniel; there is no secret that they can hide from thee: 4) With thy wisdom and with thine understanding thou has gotten thee riches, and hast gotten gold and silver into thy treasures:*

5) By thy great wisdom and by the traffic hast thou increased thy riches, and thine heart (mind) *is lifted up because of thy riches: 6) Therefore thus saith the Lord God; Because thou hast set thine heart* (mind) *as the heart* (mind) *of God; 7) Behold, therefore I will bring strangers* (barbarians) *upon thee, the terrible of the nations: and they shall draw their swords against the beauty of thy wisdom, and they shall defile thy brightness. 8) They shall bring thee down to the pit, and thou shalt die the deaths of them that are slain in the midst of the seas. 9) wilt thou yet say before him that slayeth thee, I am God? but thou shalt be a man, and no God, in the hand of him that slayeth thee. 10) Thou shalt die the deaths of the uncircumcised* (ungodly) *by the hand of strangers: for I have spoken it, saith the Lord God.*

Again we read about the rebellion of Lucifer. And turning to Rev. 12:4 we find out that Lucifer deceived one third of

Yahveh's children. *4) And his tail* (dragged down) *drew the third part of the* (now called Fallen Angels) **STARS OF HEAVEN**, *and did cast them to the Earth: and the* (Isreal) **DRAGON** *stood before the woman which was ready to be delivered, for to devour her* **CHILD** [Yahshua] *as soon as it was born.* (came to be) Skipping on to verse *7) And there* (the heavens) *was war in heaven: Michael* [another Cherub angel just as Lucifer was] *and his angels* **FOUGHT AGAINST** *the* **DRAGON**; *and the* **DRAGON** *fought and* (using) *his angels, 8) And prevailed not; neither was their place found any more in Heaven. 9) And the* **GREAT DRAGON** *was cast out, that* **OLD SERPENT**, *called the* **DEVIL**, *and* **SATAN**, *which deceiveth the whole world: he was cast out into the Earth, and his angels were cast out with him.* [v.9 has not happened yet]

This is just more proof that there was truly a **GREAT REBELLION** between Yahveh and his children, with Lucifer being the opposition. In verse 9 we have THE GREAT DRAGON, THE OLD SERPENT, THE DEVIL, and SATAN.

As I mentioned before that YAHVEH, YAHSHUA, and MELCHISEDEC are the same person, so is it with Lucifer.

He is the great dragon of Revelation, just as he is the old serpent in the garden who seduced Eve. And just as important, Lucifer will be the anti-Christ who is to come at the closing of this **SECOND WORLD AGE.**

The anti-Christ, which means instead of Christ, will be Lucifer in person, **DEFACTO**. It will not be some human being that's alive on this planet.

Don't let anyone tell you different. As it says in verse 9, *he was cast out into the Earth, and his angels were cast out with him.* This has not happened yet, but his time is coming soon.

PART FOUR: The Heavens and Earth THAT THEN WAS.

I hope by now that you have gotten a fantastic picture and a great understanding of what has happened in the first two verses of Genesis. The time that was covered in these two verses can not be known or measured, but it must of taken millions of years for Lucifer to fall as he did.

So for a little recap of the **WORLD THAT THEN WAS,** it goes like this. **YAHVEH**; the only one in existence, created first; millions of Spirit Beings that He called **HIS CHILDREN.** Yahveh then created the Heavens and the Earth. The Earth is where all of Yahveh's children dwelled. Their lives were similar to human life today, as far as having a home, a job, and also free time to enjoy for themselves. Granted their homes and jobs were not like anything we can imagine, but living in God's Kingdom and as in all Kingdoms, there were certain positions, duties, and rules, which had to be followed to enjoy a life with God. And knowing Yahveh as I do, there was no burden, frustration, or objection in His Kingdom as we find in our every day jobs and life of today.

Yahveh knows what is best for us, and He knows how to run and govern all that exists. It is only when we start thinking about ourselves that gets us into trouble, because we start doing our own will instead of Yahveh's.

He created us for His own pleasure, [Col.1:16, Rev. 4:11] and we should try to achieve this goal at all cost. To be thinking only of ourselves is to be the opposite of Him. And to be the opposite of Yahveh is to be the opposite of **LOVE.**

This was the fall of Lucifer. His position is Yahveh's government, and the beauty, knowledge, wisdom, and skill he possessed, turned him into the selfish, greedy, power hungry tyrant he is today. If Yahveh had not stopped him, he would of eventually corrupted all of Yahveh's children. This is the reason why the First World Age had to come to an end.

The horrible attitude, and hate of God, could not go on any longer. Something had to be done before this rebellious invasion infiltrated **ALL OF US.**

As I said, the First World Age came to an end. All life on this planet was destroyed. The Heavens and the Earth still existed, as did all of God's children, but there was no light. Total darkness covered all the Heavens, and the ground of the Earth was covered with water. This period of time, and we don't know how long it lasted, meet its final hour.

Now we have a predicament for Yahveh to solve. What should He do? Well the obvious answer is Yahveh should destroy Lucifer and his followers. Just because they are spirit beings that doesn't mean they can't be destroyed. They, like ourselves, are not immortal.

But would that really solve the problem? What would stop the rest of His children from corruption? Holding the sword of Death over their heads? Surely not. Yahveh created us to be free willed individuals. He wants us to love Him because we do and not out of force and fear. Nobody can truly love a dictator. Besides, if they were your children, could you kill them off?

So then what is the solution? What should Yahveh do? Well as we read in Ezek. 28:18, Lucifer will be destroyed by a consuming fire and turned into ashes. He is the only one at this time who is sure to face eternal destruction, or as written in Rev. 20:14 **THE SECOND DEATH**.

This will only happen after **ALL OF US** have been judged. There will be others destroyed along with Lucifer, but as your reading this today, he is the only one who has been already sentenced for destruction.

But what about the others? What about the one-third that Lucifer deceived into following him?

Well, His plan for them is just another reason why we should love Yahveh with all our heart. **REPENTANCE!**

Yes, God's plan for those deceived by the evil one is a chance for repentance. How is this going to be done, you ask? Enter in **FLESH AND BLOOD, THE SECOND WORLD AGE**.

All of Yahveh's children have to be born of a woman, and their essences are entombed in a Flash and Blood body.

Now before you start calling me a nut, let me prove this knowledge to you. We'll start in *Job 32:8*. It reads, *But there is a spirit in man: and the inspiration of the Almighty giveth them* (intellect) [the elect] *understanding.*

Every Human Being is actually a Spirit Being occupying a Flesh and Blood body. Turn to *Romans 9:12, It was said unto her,* [Rebecca] *The elder shall serve the younger. 13) As it is written, Jacob have I loved, but Esau have I hated.*

Now why would Yahveh love one child and hate the other? Well it's not the Little Flesh and Blood baby the Lord hated. It was the Spirit Being He placed into that body that the Lord hated. Yahveh knew beforehand the Spirit Being He put into Esau, just as He knows exactly who we ourselves really are.

Don't make the mistake believing that we come into existence the minute we are born. Turn to *Ecc.12:7* it says, *Then shall the dust* (Flesh and Blood) *return to the Earth as it was: and the Spirit* (being) *shall* **RETURN** *unto God who gave it.* To return, is to go back to a place where you have already been. We all existed way before Flesh and Blood came onto the scene.

Now let's go to *Heb. 2:14*. *Forasmuch* (Just) *then as the children are partakers of the flesh and blood, He* [Yahveh] *also Himself likewise took part of the same; that through death He might destroy him that had the power of death, that is, the devil; 15) And deliver them who through fear of death were* **ALL THEIR LIFETIME** *subject to bondage.*

Here it says even Yahveh became Flesh and Blood to prove that He, Himself, could not die, or be killed. Second, He died to set our minds free from the mystery of death, showing us that we really don't die, but continue on to a far better life. The life we look forward to! The life that we knew way before all this mess [Lucifer's rebellion] happened.

This is the reason Yahveh created Flesh and Blood, so that every child of His could experience what life is without Him. He lets you use the free will He gives us. We live as Flesh and Blood to prove to ourselves that we need His guidance and most of all, his **LOVE**.

Flesh and Blood proves how awful life is without Him and against Him.

PART FIVE: Flesh and Blood, THE SECOND WORLD AGE.

GENESIS 1:3 And God said, Let there be light:

and there was light.

This was the beginning of the "heavens and earth which are now" as written in II Peter 3:7. A whole new creation of life is about to come forth.

Now I want to make it clear to you that the earth and all the universe still existed. It was completely desolate as you read in Jer.4:23-28. But for the most part, this world and all the other planets were still present.

So, verse 3 we have light. Verses 4 & 5, Yahveh divides the light from the darkness, thus creating day and night.

Now here I would like to bring in a spiritual aspect to these verses.

You can definitely see that Yahveh is creating an environment that consists of good and evil. He didn't create evil, Lucifer did. But now, because of his rebellion, this second world age must consist of both good and evil.

All through our Bibles darkness represents Lucifer or evil. Just as Yahshua will always be known as the light of the world. *John 3:19 says, And this is the* (judgment) *condemnation, that light has come into the world, and men loved darkness rather than light, because their deeds were evil. 20) For every one that doeth evil hateth the light, neither cometh to the light, lest his deeds should be* (examined) *reproved. 21) But he that doeth truth cometh to the light, that his deeds may be made* (clear) *manifest, That they are wrought in God.*

As I said above, these verses are represented more towards the aspects of good and evil.

Yahveh here brings the light back into being. And as we have learned, Yahshua is that light of love, and Yahshua is also the **WORD** of God.

The reason I believe this is more a division of good and evil is because the sun and the moon are not created until the fourth day, whereas Yahveh's light came on day one. Even as you read on to verses 6, 7, and 8, there is still more division in a spiritual sense.

I would also like to mention how perfect God's word is.

In verse 16 Yahveh creates two great lights, one to rule the day and one to rule the night. Many times when Yahveh refers to time periods about his people, He uses the words days and or years.

When He refers to Lucifer's followers, He uses the words months and moons. So in all practical sense, the sun is Yahveh and the moon is Satan.

Now the sun is the true source of light whereas the moon is just a reflection of that light. It is a false light. An imposter of the real thing. And this is exactly what Satan is. And because of this analogy, I truly believe the Bible is the inspired word of God as written in II Tim.3:16. The word of God is so perfect that He combines life with creation. There is no way someone could write a book such as the Bible and have it intertwine with life and history as it does.

Everything in the Bible, as well as all creation, had to be perfectly planed. And only God could have done this.

So now that we all agree that the Bible is the inspired word of God, let's continue on to see what other wisdom and knowledge Yahveh has to offer us from His Scriptures.

In verses 3, 4, 5, we have light. In verse 6, 7, and 8 we have the creation of the **FIRMAMENT.**

It's hard to say exactly what the firmament is. It divided the waters from the waters. At this time, there was no ground or earth that could be seen on this planet. All was covered by water. The firmament divided the waters, so I believe there are the waters of heaven and the waters of earth. I have read other books that said at this time [before Noah's flood] the sky looked like a dome of water. So I call this dome of water: the firmament. Others call the firmament the space or expanse between the two waters. Either way, the waters above the expanse eventually were poured out onto the earth by Yahveh. And we know that as Noah's flood or the great deluge.

Okay! As we move on, Yahveh in verse 9, lets dry land appear. He calls it Earth, so I guess we should call it Earth too. Verses 11 and 12, vegetation, grasses, plants, trees. Verses 14-18 the Sun and the Moon. And in verse 20, **LIFE!**

Now this word **LIFE,** in the Hebrew text is, Nephesh (neh'-fesh. #5315 in your Strong's Concordance.) The correct word that should be translated here is **SOUL.**

Now I know some of you have been taught that we all have a soul. As a matter of fact, it's called an immortal soul. Well through time, things get twisted. I'm going to get deep here, so pay attention!

First let's start with verse *20) And God said, let the waters bring forth abundantly the moving creature that hath* (soul) **LIFE.**

As I said, this is the Hebrew word Nephesh. And properly translated into English, is the word Soul.

The definition of the word Nephesh is any creature that needs and breathes air, or to be more complex (oxygen) is a living Soul. All fish, birds, reptiles, mammals, and mankind are considered a living soul.

Now remember, I said, **ARE** a living soul, not **HAVE** a living soul. Many are taught that we all **HAVE** a soul. This is wrong; we **ARE** a soul. So just to get it straight, the word soul just means a body that breathes air to live. It doesn't matter whether it's an animal or a human being. We all are considered a living soul.

Now let's get to the part where all this soul stuff was twisted around. *Job 32:8 But there is a SPIRIT IN MAN: and the* (intellect) *inspiration of the Almighty giveth them understanding.*

This is where it all was twisted around. We were saying that man has a immortal living soul, when we should of been saying, man has an immortal spirit, living within his (body) soul.

Man has a spirit within, not a soul within. We read about this in the last chapter. (flesh and blood) *Ecc.12:7 Then shall the dust return to the earth as it was: and the SPIRIT shall return unto God who gave it.*

Let's not let Satan twist the word of God around. But wait! Is this spirit in man really an immortal spirit? Will it live on forever? Those that were taught they have an immortal soul say yes. But I'm sorry to say, the answer to that question is **NO!** We do not have an immortal soul and as a matter of fact, we don't even have an immortal spirit.

We're going to go to I Cor. 15:44. Now I'll start at verse 44, but for a greater understanding of the word of God, read the entire (Bible) chapter. (Ha Ha) (Just throwing in a little joke there. I'm funny that way.)

I Cor. 15:44 It is sown a natural body; it is raised a spiritual body. There is a natural body, and there is (also) a spiritual body. 45) And so it is written, The first man Adam was made a living soul; the last Adam [Yahshua] *was made* (into) a
(life giving)
quickening spirit. 46) Howbeit that was not first which is spiritual, but that which is natural; and afterward that which is spiritual. 47) The first man is of the (dust) *earth, earthy: the second man is the Lord from heaven. 48) As is the earthy, such are they also that are earthy: and as is the heavenly, such are they also that are heavenly. 49) And as we have borne the image of the earthy, we shall also bear the image of the heavenly.* [Those on earth consist of the dust; those in heaven consist of spirit] *50) Now this I say, brethren, that flesh and blood cannot inherit the kingdom of God; neither doth corruption inherit incorruption. 51)* (die) *Behold, I shew you a mystery; We shall not all sleep, but we shall **ALL** be changed, 52) In a moment, in the twinkling of an eye, at the last trump:* (7th trump Rev. 11:15) *for the trumpet shall sound, and the dead shall be raised incorruptible,* [raised in a spiritual body] *and we shall be changed. 53) For this*
(flesh body)   (a spiritual body)   (dying soul, body)
*corruptible must put on incorruption, and this **MORTAL** must put on immortality.*

54) So when this corruptible (flesh) *shall have put on*
(a spiritual body)
incorruption, and this mortal shall have put on immortality, (word) *then shall be brought to pass the saying that is written, Death is swallowed up in victory. 55) O death, where is thy sting? O*

grave, where is thy victory? 56) The sting of death is sin; and the strength of sin is the law. 57) But thanks be to God, which giveth us the victory through our Lord Jesus Christ. [Yahshua] *58) Therefore, my beloved brethren, be ye steadfast, unmovable, always abounding in the work of the Lord, forasmuch as ye know that your labour is not in vain in the Lord.*

Now let's recap. We are all born of flesh and blood. Our bodies are corruptible, which means they age, change, and die. But after death, we take on a new body: A spiritual body. Verse 51 says, *Behold, I shew you a mystery.* This is fantastic; Yahveh is going to tell us a secret. We shall not all sleep, but we shall all be changed, in a moment, in the twinkling of an eye, at the last trump: the last trump is the return of our Lord Jesus Christ. When this takes place, all the people who are alive on this earth shall be immediately changed from a flesh and blood body into a spiritual body.

The people who have died before hand are already in their spiritual bodies. Flesh and blood will no longer exist. The **CORRUPTIBLE** has put on **INCORRUPTION**. But now the **MORTAL** has to put on **IMMORTALITY**.

The word mortal means "able to die." So don't think that just because we now have a spiritual body that doesn't grow old and die, that you can't be destroyed.

Satan has a incorruptible body, yet he will be the first destroyed. Also if you remember earlier, before flesh and blood, we all existed in an incorruptible body. We consisted of spirit way before flesh and blood came on the scene. So believe me, we will all be very comfortable returning to those bodies.

Not only that, but we will also get back our 100% brain capabilities. We will all remember every thing that has happened since the beginning of creation.

This whole 7,000 year plan of God's is a learning process. It's purpose is to show ourselves that life without God is no life at all.

We will all be judged according to our faith and works, and we will receive the punishment or rewards we deserve.

I would like to make a personal comment at this time in regards to our judgment. I truly feel that judgment will be, for the most part, up to you the individual.

When we come back to the realization of all creation, God will ask the question: "do you or don't you want to live for eternity with the Lord?"

There will be many that will say: "no, I do not want to exist under your law or your ways." They personally would rather be turned to ash then to live a life with God.

Satan is just one of these types. All through history, men and women have had so much power in their lives that to be subjected to someone other than themselves, is much too hard to accept.

Others may have had such a great time partaking in drunkenness, drugs, or sex, that they are utterly unable to give up such sinful ways. They too would rather be destroyed then to live without their vice.

Like I said, this is my personal belief of the judgment, and in no manner or way, will I ever try to make others succumb to this belief. Now as for this book and what I have learned about Yahveh's plan for his children, that's a different story.

OK, where were we before I want off on a mind trip? Oh yeah, immortality! This will take place at the great judgment, and it will be either life forever with Yahveh, or the second death as written in Rev.20. It's that simple.

Now let's go way back to where we were talking about life! Verses 20, 21, and 22, Yahveh is creating all the creatures of the seas and all the birds of the air. In Verses 24 and 25, we have Yahveh creating all the wild beasts and the other creatures of the earth. And in Verses 26, 27, and 28, we have the creation of **MANKIND**.

I would like to add one thing to all the above verses. Yahveh makes it a point in telling us that all He creates multiples after its own kind. Meaning, there is in no way that the belief of evolution is true. When He repeats verses such as these, get it through your head! Everything multiplied after their own kind. The Bible offers more proof against evolution than there is for evolution. Now, back to **MANKIND**.

Gen.1:26 And God said, Let us make man in our image, after our likeness: and let **THEM** *have dominion over the fish of the sea, and over the fowl of the air, and over the cattle, and over all the earth, and over every creeping thing that creepeth upon the earth. 27) So God created man in His own image, in the image of God created he him;* **MALE AND FEMALE** *created he* **THEM**. *28) And God blessed* **THEM**, *and God said unto* **THEM**, *Be fruitful,* (fill again) *and multiply, and replenish the earth, and subdue it: and have dominion over the fish of the sea, and over the fowl of the air, and over every living thing that moveth upon the earth.*

This is a very important part of Genesis. The creation of **MANKIND**. I don't know about you, but I was taught that Adam and Eve were the first two human beings made by God. And that all of mankind was brought forth by them. Well I hate to say it, but again this information is **WRONG**!

Let's start with verse 26. *And God said, Let us make man in our image, after our likeness.* The word **MAN** in the Hebrew is #120 in the Strong's, and it means **MANKIND**: Not just one man, but many. They will be made in the image of God and after His likeness.

This means man will have the same body form that Yahveh has. And then it says, in His likeness, this means, without sin.

All of mankind was created sinless. They were all made with a pure heart. They had no evil thoughts or perversion. Mankind was made in the perfect likeness of God. *27) So God created man* (mankind) *in his own image, in the image of God created he him; **MALE and FEMALE** created he **THEM**.* It's very obvious that there is more than one person being created here! Not only that, but both male and female are being created at the same time. *Verse 28) And God blessed **THEM**, And God said unto **THEM**, Be fruitful, and multiply, and* (fill again) *replenish the earth, and subdue it.*

There is no doubt in my mind that Yahveh has created more than one person here.

And just to throw in a little extra proof that this is the second world age, That word "replenish" means **TO FILL AGAIN**. You cannot fill something again unless it first has been emptied. So what we have here is that all the different races of mankind were created on the sixth day. (verse 31)

Now I would also like to address the question about what we are to eat. Verse 29 and 30 say that Yahveh has given us, and all the creatures of this world, every herb, plant, and fruit tree to us for food.

Now what about meat? Are we to eat meat or refrain from it? Let's go to *Gen. 9:3* it reads. *Every moving thing that liveth shall be meat for you; even as the green herb have I given you all things.* And if we turn to *I Tim.4:1-5* it says, *Now the* (Holy) *Spirit speaketh expressly, that in the* ***LATTER TIMES*** [NOW] *some shall depart from the faith* (in Christ) *giving heed to seducing spirits, and* (religions) *doctrines of devils; 2) Speaking lies in hypocrisy; having their conscience* (branded) *seared* (Satan's) *with a hot iron; 3)* ***FORBIDDING TO MARRY***, *and commanding to* ***ABSTAIN FROM MEATS***, *which God hath created to be received with thanksgiving of them which* ***BELIEVE AND KNOW THE TRUTH***. *4) For every creature of God is good, and nothing to be refused, if it be received with thanksgiving: 5) For it is sanctified by the* ***WORD*** *of God and prayer.*

Well, as we just read, eating meat does not go against the word of God. And for a little more proof, let's go to *Matt.15:11, 17-20. 11) Not that which goeth into the mouth defileth a man; but that which cometh out of the mouth, this defileth a man. 17) Do not ye yet understand, that whatsoever entereth in at the mouth goath into the belly, and is cast out into the draught? 18) But those things which proceed out of the mouth come forth from the* (mind) *heart; and they defile the man. 19) For out of the* (mind) *heart proceed evil thoughts, murders, adulteries, fornications, thefts, false witness, blasphemies! 20) These are the things which defile a man: but to eat with unwashen hands defileth not a man.*

It's plain to see that we can eat just about everything that moves on this earth. As a matter of fact, we usually do. But I do want to mention that the reason Yahveh told us not to eat certain meats is because they are scavengers, and these types of creatures eat the poisons and rot of the world. Eating them may cause sickness or even death. Lev.11 explains this deeper, if you're interested.

OK, back to **MANKIND**. Chapter two starts out, *Thus the heavens and the earth* **[WHICH ARE NOW]** *were finished, and all the* **HOST** *of them.* The **HOST** that is mentioned here are God's children that He would be sending down to earth to go through this flesh and blood, **SECOND WORLD AGE**.

Yahveh had at this time a list of everyone needing to learn the important lesson, that life without Him; or for that matter, against Him, was the worst thing in existence. Us being here today was planned by Yahveh at least 6,000 years ago.

Verse 2 should obviously read *And on the* **SIXTH DAY** *God ended his work which he had made; and he rested on the* **SEVENTH DAY** *from all his work which he had made.* I would like to mention that Yahveh rested from His achievement and not from fatigue, as man has to do. In Verse 3, God blesses the seventh day.

Verse 4 God verifies what He has done. And now verse 5 is the shocker: *THERE WAS NOT A MAN TO TILL THE GROUND.*

This I believe is an **EIGHTH DAY** creation. Yahveh already created male and female to have dominion over the fish of the sea. They are known as fishermen.

Yahveh also had male and female to have dominion over the fowl of the air and the beasts of the earth. They are known as hunters. But as for the plants of the fields, Yahveh did not have a farmer. There was not a man to till the ground. So as I mentioned in verse 7 it reads, *AND THE LORD GOD FORMED MAN OF THE DUST OF THE GROUND, AND BREATHED INTO HIS NOSTRILS THE BREATH OF LIFE: AND MAN BECOME A LIVING SOUL*.

Now there are two words here that I would like to investigate.

The first is the word **FORMED**. Back in chapter 1 verse 27, it says that God **CREATED** man. That word created is #1254 in the Strong's. The men and women that were made on the sixth day came into existence by miracle. Meaning, God said, Let there be man, and there was man. But for the eighth day creation, it says that God **FORMED** man of the dust.

The word formed is #3335 in the Strong's. It means that God formed this man like a potter. Yahveh took the dust of the ground and molded him with His hands, just as a potter does with clay. This man was not produced by miracle. He was made personally by Yahveh Himself.

Now the reason God did this was that the race of man He was creating here would some day in a future generation have our Lord Jesus Christ born out of him. Yahveh knew beforehand, that through this man's loins would some day come Yahshua, who would die on a cross for all the sins of mankind. Yahveh didn't make His plans as time went by. This was a plan that was finished before it started. God is that perfect! **AMEN**!

Now let's go on to the word **MAN**. And the Lord God formed **MAN** of the dust of the ground. This word **MAN** is #121 in the Strong's. The Hebrew has it, eth-ha adham meaning, the man named Adam. #120 is mankind, #121 is the man named Adam. These are the little things that get so turned around.

I like to say that it's not a man's fault the truth gets twisted around; it's Satan's fault. He's the one who doesn't want us to know the truth. He's the one who leads us to stray. He's the one who tempts us. And he's the one who started this whole mess in the first place. Well enough about him, let's get back to Adam.

In verse 8, we have Yahveh giving Adam a place to live. And in verse 9, we have the **TREE OF LIFE** and the **TREE OF KNOWLEDGE** of good and evil. Well I hate to say it, but here we go again.

Many times in God's word, trees represent people. If you did any of the studies, you have found out for yourself that this is true. But for those of you who haven't, I'll go into it a little bit.

The tree of life represents Yahshua. The tree of the knowledge of good and evil represents Satan. In *Mark 8:24* it says, *And he looked up, and said, I see men as trees, walking.* In
Isaiah 61:3 To appoint ^(assign) *unto them that mourn in Zion, to give unto them beauty for ashes, the oil of joy for mourning, the garment of praise for the spirit of heaviness; that they might be called* **TREES OF RIGHTEOUSNESS**, *the planting of the Lord, that he might be glorified.*

To Yahveh, His people are trees of righteousness. And how do you know if someone is of God or Satan? It's by their fruits, which means the work they do, the way they conduct themselves, and basically, the manner in which they live. Let's go to *Matt. 7:15 Beware of false prophets, which come to you in sheep's clothing, but inwardly they are* ravening ^(hungry) *wolves. 16) Ye* shall know them by their fruits. Do men gather grapes of thorns, or figs of thistles? 17) Even so every good tree bringeth forth good fruit; but a corrupt tree bringeth forth evil fruit. 18) A good tree cannot bring forth evil fruit, neither can a corrupt tree bring forth good fruit.

19) Every tree that bringeth not forth good fruit is hewn down, and cast into the fire. 20) Wherefore **BY THEIR FRUITS YE SHALL KNOW THEM**.

And in Matt.12:33 Either make a tree good, and his fruit good; or else make the tree corrupt, and his fruit corrupt: for the tree is known by his fruit. As you can see, it's not too hard to tell if a man is of God or of Satan.

Now I'm going to the book of Judges. Here we will read about people being represented by all types of different trees. Let's start at Judges 9:7 And when they told it to Jotham, he went and stood in the top of mount Gerizim, and lifted up his voice, and cried, and said unto them, Hearken unto me, ye men of Shechem, that God may hearken unto you. 8) The **TREES** (people) went forth on a time to anoint a king over them; and they said unto the olive tree [Israel's religious privileges], Reign (rule) thou over us. 9) But the olive tree said unto them, Should I leave my fatness, wherewith by me they honour God and man, and go to be promoted (king) over the trees (people)? 10) and the trees (people) said to the fig tree [Israel's national privileges], Come thou, and reign (rule) over us. 11) But the fig tree said unto them, Should I forsake my sweetness, and my good fruit, and go to be promoted (king) over the trees (people)? 12) Then said the trees (people) unto the vine [Israel's spiritual privileges], Come thou, and reign (rule) over us. 13) And the vine said unto them, Should I leave my wine, which cheereth God and man,

and go to be   promoted^(king) over the trees?^(people) 14) Then said all the
trees^(people) unto the bramble,^(Satan) Come thou, and reign^(rule) over us. 15) And
the bramble^(Satan) said unto the trees,^(people) If in truth ye anoint me king

over you, then come and put your trust in my shadow: [Bramble

doesn't cast a shadow] and if not, let fire come out of the bram-

ble, and devour the cedars of Lebanon [people of God].

As we just read, trees sometimes do represent people. And

this last one, **CEDARS OF LEBANON**, is used many times in the

word of God. It will always represent the people of God.

Now let's go to *Ezek. 31:3 Behold, the Assyrian^(Satan) was a cedar

in Lebanon with fair^(beautiful) branches, and with a shadowing shroud^(foliage),

and of an high stature; and his top was among the thick boughs.*

4) The waters made him great, the deep set him up on high

with her rivers running round about his plants, and sent out her

little rivers unto all the trees^(men) of the field. [Isaiah 14:8] *5)*

Therefore his height was exalted above all the trees^(men) of the

field, and his boughs were multiplied, and his branches became

long because of the multitude of waters, when he shot forth. 6)

All the fowls of heaven made their nests in his boughs,^(arms) and

under his branches did all the beasts of the field bring forth

their young, and under his shadow dwelt all great nations. 7)

Thus was he fair in his greatness, in the length of his branches:

for his root was by great waters. 8) The cedars in the garden of

God could not hide him: the fir trees were not like his boughs,

and the chestnut trees were not like his branches; nor any tree

in the garden of God was like unto him in his beauty. [Satan was

the most beautiful of all.] *9) I have made him fair by the multi-*

tude of his branches: so that all the trees of Eden, that were in

the garden of God, envied him [Lucifer]. *10) Therefore thus saith* the Lord God; Because thou hast lifted up thyself in height, and he hath shot up his top among the thick boughs, and his heart is lifted up in his height; 11) I have therefore delivered him into the hand of the mighty one of the heathen (nations) he shall surely deal with him:

I have driven him out (of Eden) for his wickedness. 12) And strangers, the terrible of the nations, have I cut him off, and have left him: upon the mountains and in all the valleys his branches are fallen, and his boughs are broken by all the rivers of the land; and all the people of the earth are gone down from his shadow, and have left him. 13) Upon his ruin shall all the fowls of the heaven remain, and all the beasts of the field shall be upon his branches: 14) To the end that none of all the (men) trees by the waters exalt themselves for their height, neither shoot up their top among the thick boughs, neither their trees stand up in their height, all that drink water: for they are all delivered unto death, to the (lower) nether parts of the earth, in the midst of the chil- dren of (Adam) men, with them that go down to the pit. 15) Thus saith the Lord God; In the day when he went down to the grave I caused a mourning: I covered the (seas) deep for him and I restrained the floods thereof, and the great waters were (stopped) stayed: **AND I** [Yahveh] caused (God's people) Lebanon to mourn for him, and all the trees of the field fainted for him. 16) I made the nations to shake at the sound of his fall, when I cast him down to (the grave) hell with them that descend into the pit: and all the (mankind) trees of Eden, the choice and best of Lebanon, all that drink water, shall be comforted in the (lower) nether parts of the earth.

17) They also went down into (the grave) hell with him unto them that be slain with the sword; and they that were his (seed) arm, that dwelt

under his shadow in the midst of the heathen. 18) To whom art thou thus like in glory and in greatness among the trees of Eden? Yet shalt thou be brought down with the trees of Eden unto the nether parts of the earth: thou shalt lie in the midst of the uncircumcised with them that be slain by the ^(truth) *sword.*

Now much of this is for Satan and his children. Again we just read what will happen to him. But for the children of God let's go to *Hosea 14:4. I will heal their backsliding, I will love them freely: for mine anger is turned away from him. 5) I will be as the dew unto Israel: he shall grow as the lily, and cast forth his roots as* (the cedars of) *Lebanon.*

6) His branches shall spread, and his beauty shall be as the olive tree, and his smell as (cedar) *Lebanon. 7) They that dwell under his shadow shall return; they shall revive as the corn, and grow as the vine: the scent thereof shall be as the wine of* (cedar) *Lebanon.*

8) Ephraim shall say, What have I to do any more with idols? I have heard him, and observed him: I am like a (evergreen) *green fir tree. From me is thy fruit found. 9) Who is wise, and* (who) *he shall understand these things? prudent, and he shall know them? for the ways of the Lord was right, and the just shall walk in them: but the transgressors shall fall therein.*

So I guess it's safe for me to say that Yahveh likes using trees to represent man, or His people, or as we started this study, His son Yahshua.

If you turn to *Rev. 2:7 He that hath an ear, let him hear what the* (Holy) *Spirit saith unto the churches; To him that over-* (PARTAKE) *cometh will I give to **EAT** of the tree of life* [Yahshua] *which is* (gardens) *in the midst of the paradise of God.*

As you just read, I used the word "**PARTAKE**," in place of eat. This is important for understanding the next major study. We do not eat of the tree of life; we partake of His fruits. And we should all know by now what that means. We partake of Yahshua's way of life, His essence, love, and mercy. We should all want to be as He is. We should be doing the work He wants us to to: Partaking in righteousness and not sin.

If you turn to *John 6:25-65,* and it say's, **YAHSHUA** *is the bread of life. (35, 48)* It is a spiritual food we need. And that my friends is the fruit to partake of. The fruit that offers us eternal life. The fruit from the **TREE OF LIFE**.

Now to continue on, let's get back to Adam. He's been put in a garden of Eden. Which has the Tree of life, and also the tree of the knowledge of good and evil.

Verse 15 say's, Adam was put there to cultivate and keep it. And in verse 16 it says, *And the Lord God commanded the man,* [Adam] *saying, Of every tree of the garden thou mayest freely* **EAT***:* (PARTAKE) *17) But of the tree of the knowledge of good and evil,* [Satan] *thou shalt not eat* (partake) *of it: for* **IN THE DAY** *that thou eatest* (partake) *thereof thou shalt surely die.* Adam did partake, and he did not last one day with the Lord. [See note on p. 20]

In verse 18 it says, *It is not good that the man* [Adam] *should be alone;.* This is just another example of proof that Adam was not the first man.

In chapter 1:27, 28, it say's *God created male and female, God blessed them.* But here in 2:18 Adam is alone. And in verse *19 And out of the* **GROUND** *the Lord God* **FORMED** *every beast of the field.*

Now I would like to mention that these animals formed here are a separate group of animals. Since Adam is a farmer, it's safe to say that these animals are the domesticated farm animals we have today.

The animals created in chapter 1 are the wild animals, but these animals for Adam are farm animals. Just as their are two separate creations of man, there are two separate creations of animals.

Now to continue, verses 21-25 show the creation of Adam's wife.

The word in verse 21, **RIB**, should be a curve or a chunk. Just as a potter can take the clay from one project and start another, so was it with the forming of Adam and his wife Eve.

OK, now we come to the chapter in which truth again has been twisted around. *Chapter 3 Now the serpent* (Satan) *was more subtil* (wiser) *than any beast of the field which the Lord God had made. And he* [Satan] *said unto the woman, Yea, hath God said, Ye shall not eat of every tree of the garden?* Right here, the first words out of Satan's mouth twist the truth around. Yahveh said, you **CAN** eat of all the trees except one. Lucifer said, you can't eat of the trees of the garden. Lucifer misquoted Yahveh on purpose to make Eve think twice.

As you can probably see, Lucifer is after Eve. Why you say? Well it's because Satan knows that through Eve will come the Messiah, whose job it will be to destroy Satan and all his evil works. If he can destroy the woman, he can stop the coming of our Lord, Yahshua.

This is the reason Yahveh calls a certain group His chosen people. And for us, the Bible is a record of those people.

Now, let's get back to Eve. *2) And the woman said unto the serpent,* **WE** [Adam present] *may eat* (partake) *of the fruit of the trees of the garden: 3) But of the fruit of the tree which is in the midst of the garden, God hath said, Ye shall not eat* (partake) *of it, neither shall ye* **TOUCH** *it, lest you die. 4) And the serpent said unto the woman, Ye shall not surely die:*

Here is the second sentence out of the mouth of Satan, and again it's a lie, or at least, a good twisting of the truth. Now I also would like to address the word **TOUCH**, in verse 3.

Again I was always taught that Adam and Eve ate an apple from the tree of good and evil. I'm sure you were taught the same. Well I hate to say it, but again we have been told a lie. Let's go to verse *13, And the Lord God said unto the woman, What is this that thou hast done? And the woman said, The serpent* **BEGUILED** *me, and I did eat.* (partake)

Now we have the word **TOUCH** and the word **BEGUILED**. The word touch is #5060 in the Strong's, and the word beguiled is #5377. Both of these words mean to seduce in a sexual way. To put it bluntly, Lucifer had sexual relations with Eve. Now that is far from the belief of an apple being eaten. I'll take you even further. Turn to *II Cor. 11:3* it say's *But I fear, lest by any means, as the serpent* **BEGUILED** *Eve through his* (craftiness) *subtilty, so your minds should be corrupted from the simplicity that is in Christ.*

This word beguiled is #1818 of the Greek text, in the Strong's. It also means **TO WHOLLY SEDUCE** in a sexual way.

Do you understand what happened in the garden? Satan seduced and took part in Adam and Eve's first sexual relation. Call it an orgy, threesome, or whatever. But believe me, a sexual affair took place.

Now this I could understand would make Yahveh much more angry than eating some kind of forbidden fruit.

And for a little more proof, go back to *Gen. 3:15* it say's, *And I* [Yahveh] *will put enmity between* (Satan) *thee and the woman, and between* (Satan's children) *thy seed and* (Eve's children) *her seed; it shall bruise thy head,* [Future: Yahshua shall destroy Lucifer.] *and thou shall bruise his heel.* [Cause man to fall into sin.] *16) Unto the woman He said, I will greatly multiply thy sorrow and the* **CONCEPTION**; *in* (pain) *sorrow thou shalt bring forth children; and thy desire shall be to thy husband, and he shall rule over thee.*

What more proof can you ask for? Why would Yahveh greatly increase the pain of giving birth if it was just an apple or some kind of fruit they ate? This punishment was definitely caused by the sexual relations they just had. And to make it clearer, go to *4:1. And Adam knew Eve his wife; and she conceived, and bare CAIN, and said, I have gotten a man from the Lord. 2) And she* (continued to) *again bare his* (fraternal) *brother Abel. And Abel was a keeper of sheep, but Cain was a tiller of the ground.*

Now I know it's hard to believe, but Eve was impregnated by both; Lucifer and Adam. It is called a fraternal pregnancy. And I will prove this hidden information to you.

First of all, look at the names and occupations they have. Abel is a keeper of sheep. This is definitely a type of Christ. Meaning, just as Yahshua is known as the good shepherd, always searching for the lost (man) sheep. Just as King David, Abel was a shepherd, and he also is a type of Christ. But when you look at Cain, his future generations are known as Kenites, sons of Cain. They have been enemies of God's people all through history.

For more poof of this, let's go to *I John 3:11, 12* it say's *For this is the message that ye heard from the beginning, that we should love one another. 12) Not as Cain, **WHO WAS OF** (Satan) **THAT WICKED ONE**. and slew his brother. And* (why) *wherefore* (fruits) *slew he him? Because his own **WORKS** were evil, and his brother's righteous.*

Verse 12 tells it to you in plain English, Cain was of Satan, that wicked one. Turn to *John 8:42 Jesus said unto them, If God were your Father, ye would love me: for I proceeded forth and came from God; neither came I of myself, but He sent me. 43) Why do ye not understand my speech? Even because ye cannot* (message) *hear my word. 44) Ye are of your **FATHER** the **DEVIL**, and the lusts of your **FATHER** ye will do. He was a **MURDERER** from the beginning,* (of mankind) *and abode not in the truth, because there is no truth in him. When he speaketh a lie, he speaketh of his own: for he is a liar, and the father of it.*

There you have it. What more proof do you want? Cain was most assuredly the son of Lucifer, and Abel was a son of God.

So then, what do we have here? Well I'll tell you. We have Lucifer's children on one side growing. And we have Yahveh's children growing on the other side. Well actually, we have them growing along, side by side. And to prove this just a little bit more, let's go to Matt. 13, The Parable of the Sower.

1) The same day went Jesus out of the house, and sat by the sea side. 2) And great multitudes were gathered together unto him, so that he went into a ship, and sat; and the whole multitude stood on the shore. 3) And he spake many things unto them in parables, saying, Behold, a sower [A teacher of the word of (teach) God] *went forth to sow; 4) And when he sowed, some seeds* [words of God] *fell by the way side, and the fowls came and devoured them up: 5) Some fell upon stony places, where they had not much earth:* [were not buried very deep] *and forthwith* (immediately) *they sprung up, because they had no deepness of earth: 6) And when the sun was up, they were scorched; and because they had no root, they withered away. 7) And some fell among thorns; and the thorns sprung up, and choked them: 8) But other fell into good ground, and brought forth fruit, some an hundredfold, some sixty-fold, some thirtyfold. 9) Who hath ears to hear, let him hear. 10) And the disciples came, and said unto him, Why speakest thou unto them in parables? 11) He answered and said unto them, Because it is* **GIVEN UNTO YOU TO KNOW THE MYSTERIES OF THE KINGDOM OF HEAVEN**, *but to them it is* **NOT GIVEN**. *12) For whosoever hath, to him shall be given, and he shall have more abundance: but whosoever hath not, from him shall be taken away even that he hath. 13) Therefore speak I to them in parables; because they seeing see not; and hearing they hear not, neither do they understand. 14) And in them is fulfilled the prophecy of Isaiah* [Isa.6:9,10] *which saith, By hearing ye shall hear, and shall not understand; and seeing ye shall see, and shall not perceive: 15) For this people's heart is* (callous) *waxed gross, and their ears are dull of hearing, and their eyes they have closed; lest at any time they should see with their eyes, and hear with their ears, and should understand with their* (mind) *heart, and should be converted,* [be turned to the Lord] *and I should heal them. 16) But blessed are your eyes, for they see: and your ears, for they hear. 17) For verily I say unto you, That many prophets and righteous men have desired to see those things which ye see, and have* not seen them; and to hear those things which ye hear and have not heard them. 18) Hear ye therefore the parable of the sower. 19) When any one heareth the word of the kingdom, and understandeth it not, then cometh the wicked one, and catcheth away that which was sown in his heart. This is he which received seed by the way side. 20) But he that received the seed into stony places, the same is he that heareth the word, and anon (immediately) with joy receiveth it; 21) Yet hath joy he not root in him- self, but dureth (does) for a while: for when tribulation or persecu- tion ariseth because of the word (truth), by and by he is offended (stumbles).

22) He also that received seed among the thorns is he that heareth the word (truth); and the care of this world; and the deceit- fulness of riches, choke the word (truth), and he becometh unfruitful.

23) But he that received seed into the good ground is he that heareth the word (truth), and understandeth it; which also beareth fruit, and bringeth forth, some an hundredfold, some sixty, some thirty.

Now this next parable is the one I would like us to focus on. It has a lot to do with Satan's seed and God's children.

24) Another parable put he forth unto them, saying, The kingdom of heaven is likened unto a man which sowed good seed in his field: 25) But while men slept, his **ENEMY** came and sowed **TARES** (weeds) among the wheat, and went his way. 26) But when the blade (wheat) was sprung up, and brought forth fruit, then appeared the tares (weeds) also. 27) So the ser- vants of the householder came and said unto him, Sir, didst not thou sow good seed in thy field? from whence (where) then hath it tares? 28) He said unto them, An **ENEMY** hath done this. The servants said unto him, Wilt thou then that (should) we go and gather them up? 29) But he said, Nay; lest while ye gather up the tares, ye root up also the

wheat with them. *30) Let **BOTH** grow together until the **HAR-VEST**: and in the time of harvest I will say to the reapers, Gather ye together first the tares, and bind them in bundles to burn them: but gather the wheat into* (The Kingdom) *my barn. 31) Another parable put he forth unto them, saying, The kingdom of heaven is like to a grain of mustard seed, which a man took, and sowed in his field: 32) Which indeed is the* (smallest) *least of all seeds: but when it is grown, it is the* (largest) *greatest among herbs, and becometh a tree, so that the birds of the air come and lodge in the branches thereof.*

33) Another parable spake he unto them; The kingdom of heaven is like unto (sour dough) *leaven, which a woman took, and hid in three measures of meal, till the whole was* (corrupted) *leavened. 34) All these things spake Jesus unto the multitude in parables; and* (to the disciples) *without a parable spake he not unto them:* [Mark4:33,34]

35) That it might be fulfilled which was spoken by the prophet, [Isaiah 6:9,10 Ps.78:2] *saying, I will open my mouth in parables; I will utter things which have been kept **SECRET*** (since) *from the* (overthrow) *foundation of the (1st) world* (age). Verses 34 and 35 are fulfilled prophecies of the Old Testament by Yahshua Messiah.

36) Then Jesus sent the multitude away, and went into the house: and his (students) *disciples came unto him, saying,* (explain) *Declare unto us the **PARABLE OF THE TARES** of the field. 37) He answered and said unto them, He that sowed the good* (wheat) *seed is the Son of man;* [Yahshua] *38) The field is* (this world age) *the world; the good seed are the children of the* (God) *Kingdom; but the tares are the children of the wicked one; 39) The enemy that sowed them is the devil; the*

128

harvest is the end of the (next) *world* (Age) [The Millennium] *and the reapers are the angels.*

40) As therefore the tares are gathered and burned in the fire; so shall it be in the end of this world. [The 3rd world Age called the Millennium] *41) The Son of man* (Yahshua) *shall send forth* **HIS ANGELS**, *and they shall gather out of* **HIS KINGDOM** *all things that offend, and them which do iniquity; 42) And shall cast them into a furnace of fire: there shall be wailing and gnashing of teeth.* This is the second death. All evil will be burned to ash.

This is an eternal **PUNISHMENT**, not eternal **PUNISHING**. Burning in a Hell Fire for eternity is a myth. The second death is an eternal punishment of non-existence. Evil has been blotted out of life.

43) Then shall the righteous shine forth as the sun in the kingdom of their Father. (Yahveh)

Who hath ears to hear, let him hear.

Now I think there is plenty of proof here in these verses, that let us know; Satan had sexual relations with Eve, and that Cain was an offspring of that conception. Yahveh is very clear of the fact that there are two separate generations coming from the womb of Eve. Verses 4:16-24 tell us exactly the generations of Cain. Whereas verses 5:3-32 tell us the generations of Adam.

This is very important information when trying to understand God's Word; the Bible. You have Yahveh's children growing alongside Satan's children. This is the whole point of the parable about the wheat and the tares. Let them grow together until the harvest. Then gather up the tares and burn them. I'm telling you the Word of God is so perfect. Not only that; but it is easy enough that a child can understand.

Don't let the so called super intelligent theologians and philosophers tell you it's too hard to understand.

How come they never told us about what happened in the garden? Surely it's as plain as the nose on our face. Well, I guess it's wrong for me to blame them for the false beliefs. As a matter of fact, I myself, am to blame.

Why have I, all my life, trusted someone else to tell me what the Bible says. When I stand before Yahveh at the final judgment, do you think I will have a good defense by saying; Well that's what they told me, or how was I suppose to know? I think not.

The Bible is a personal letter to everyone. Isn't it better to read the letter yourself, then to let someone else read it to you? Well, I know what your thinking. Some will say that I am doing the same by writing this book. You're telling us what the Bible says. How are you any different? Well, to tell you the truth, I'm not much different then the others; except, I don't want you to just listen, or to just read this book. I want you to dig into your own Bible and get totally involved with your search for Truth.

I have listened to many teachers, and have read many books on the subject. The whole idea is to slowly weed out or add to your own personal belief. We all have to go through the process slowly and patiently to find the truth. Nobody I know, knew from the start, that one and one equals two. It must be proven to you in order to believe it. Such is the Word of God. *Prove all things; hold fast* (keep) *that which is good.* [I Thes.5:21]

I wrote this book to get you excited about God's Word, to stimulate your mind, and to ask the question we all should ask ourselves. Why do I believe what I do? or, Why am I here? What is the point of life? What happens when we die? For when these questions are answered and found to be true, then can you say I am free from the bonds of death and deception.

In *John 8:31,32* it says, *If ye continue in my word, then are ye my* (students) *disciples indeed; 32) and ye shall know the truth, and* **THE TRUTH SHALL MAKE YOU FREE.**

And once you know the truth, no man can take it away. They can take your earthy life, all your possessions, even your loved ones, but the truth, no man can take.

OK, now that that's off my chest, let's get back to Cain and Abel. As we just read, Cain is of Satan, Abel is of God. So it is not very surprising that in verse 4:9 Cain; jealous and angry, rises up and kills; no wait! **MURDERS**, his fraternal twin brother. [If you read page 73 and 74 then you already know how I feel about this word; murder.] Verse 9, Yahveh asks Cain, *Where is Abel thy brother? And he* [Cain] *said I KNOW NOT: Am I my brother's keeper?*

This is a strait out lie to the face of God. Just as Satan lies, so did Cain his son. Verse 11, Yahveh curses the ground he walks on, and Cain is driven out of his homeland.

Now I don't want to go into detail about this, but Cain's children will eventually occupy the land which is north. This land today is Russia. Our Bibles mention the people of the north many times. And when it does, always remember, it's the land that Cain's offspring occupies.

Don't take this bit of information wrong. There are many good Christians in Russia. Like a church, a country can have many good, God fearing people. It's the government, or as in a church, the organizations, that destroy the people.

When God is taken out of a country, despair, violence, and destruction takes His place. This is what is happening in America.

Atheists are people who don't believe there is a God. That's their choice. But when these people and their organizations try to get our cities, towns and government to take off religious symbols or words, most of which claiming Jesus Christ as Lord, they have now changed themselves into a type of anti-Christ.

Our Bible does mention the soon coming anti-Christ, but more important today is the attitude of an anti-Christ. It's sad that someone can be so blind to the truth.

Adultery and homosexuality we're told should be accepted as normal behavior. If it is, how come Yahveh destroyed Sodom and Gomorrah? These people are not immoral. They, like so many of our children today are, "**AMORAL**." They don't know right from wrong.

The main point that I am trying to make is: our country is sliding further and further away from the truth. You want to know why we have record floods? Why so many earthquakes, hurricanes, tornadoes, and fire? **LOOK AT SOCIETY!** Yahveh is not, I repeat, is not going to let His people plunge into this kind of transgressions. He never has and He never will.

Look what happened to His people as soon as they left Egypt lead by Moses. Yahveh destroyed many of them. Why? Because they could not handle freedom. They ran amuck. They did whatever they wanted to. And America, if it's attitude doesn't change, will suffer the same fate.

And since I'm airing it all out, I would like to address the movie and music industries. They too are a big part of our falling away.

Today, movies and television bombard us with sex and violence. Fifty years ago, it was unheard-of and shocking, to be killed on the street for ten dollars, or even more shocking, to be murdered for the clothes on your back. But today, it happens all the time.

Fifty years ago, life was precious. But today, the attitude towards life is at an all time low. Movies and television are showing our children how to be angry and violent. They see twice as much hatred and negativity than they see love. They are learning to fight with a gun, instead of understanding. Kill and destroy a problem, instead of working it out. If you want the bottom line, it's still the same old story that has destroyed countries and civilizations of the past. And that is: **WHAT I WANT I GET**.

Just about everything we see and listen to revolves around greed, lust, and violence. If you ask the entertainment businesses why do they put out such negativity, the answer is usually: that's what the people want to see. Well, if that is true, then this country doesn't have a chance.

It's too late to change the attitude of the adult. And if it's too late for the adult, then it's definitely too late for their children.

If you had to pick the one thing that is forced upon us the most, it would have to be sex. Would you like to know why our children are having sex so soon in life? Why so many teen-age pregnancies?

Well it's because of the movie and music industries. If we went back say, two hundred years, how do you think most people found out about sex. Well it was mostly, word of mouth.

Talking to each other was probably the most popular way to stimulate sexual urges. There were also paintings and statues, but for young children to see such things, it was difficult and possibly hidden from them. Another way was to witness two older adults in the act. This too would stimulate sexual urges and questions. But for the most part, all young adults went through puberty the normal way, which is brought on by time.

But for a child of the 1990's and beyond, they are forced into sexual stimulations by music videos, movies, and commercial ads: all aimed at the adults, but viewed and picked up by the children. All these sexual innuendoes and overtones trigger false urges much too early for children to comprehend and understand.

Today we all hear and read many stories about children 5 and 6 years old raping girls in their classroom. Or even worse, children killing children.

How can a child do such a thing? Well I say nine out of ten times, they saw it on television or in a movie.

So, next time you hear on the **NEWS** (which is sometimes just as bad as all the other programming,) that a child has been taken into custody for a crime, believe me, they got the idea from our entertainment industry. They are truly to blame.

Well my whole point of this opinion was to show you some of the reasons why Yahveh will punish or destroy a nation. The further away we stray, the less the blessings there shall be.

And I'll tell you right now, the greatest sin of all that this country **PARTAKES OF** is **ABORTION**. Any nation that puts a man in jail for destroying, say, Condor eggs, but has so-called doctors who destroy **HUMAN LIFE** daily, that nation is not of God and will soon be consumed by His wrath.

Well I'm sorry if I depressed you in any way, but truth is truth. Yahveh will deal with America in the manner He chooses. And for those who know and stay in His word, I'll comfort you with *Luke 21:17. And ye shall be hated of all men for my name's sake. 18) But there shall not an hair of your head perish. 19) In your patience possess ye your soul.*

And in the same chapter verse *36) Watch ye therefore, and pray always, that ye may be accounted worthy to escape all these things that shall come to pass, and to stand before the Son of man.*

Now, back to where we left off. Cain has been driven out of his homeland, and in 4:25 Eve gives birth to Seth, which means compensation.

Now Chapter five goes through the generations of Adam up until Noah. And then we come to Chapter six.

This chapter is very interesting and again you will learn about things we were never told.

Chapter six goes back to the time of Adam. *6:1 And it came to pass, when men began to multiply on the face of the earth, and daughters were born unto them. 2) That the* (angels) *sons of God saw the daughters of men that they were* (beautiful) *fair; and they took them wives of all which they chose.*

The sons of God that are mentioned here are fallen angels. Now I have mentioned that all of Yahveh's children had to be born of a woman, and go through the flesh and blood, 2nd world age. Well the spirit beings mentioned in verse 2 did not do this. They came straight to earth without being born of woman.

Let's read about it in *Jude 6) And the angels which kept not their first estate, but left their own habitation,* [heaven]   *He* (God has them now)   (until) *hath reserved in everlasting chains under darkness unto the judgment of the great day.*

These spirit beings came down to earth and were having sexual intercourse with any woman they chose. Now I'm sure you have never heard of such a thing, but this is what took place here.

In verse 4, we have more poof of this. *There were **GIANTS** in the earth in those days; and also after that,* [the flood] *when* (fallen angels) *the sons of God came in unto the daughters of men, and they **BARE CHILDREN** to them, the same became mighty men which were of old, men of renown.*

These offspring are known as Nephilim, which means fallen ones. This is the reason Yahveh brought to pass the great flood. The Nephilim were not only great in size, but also very evil, abnormal, and possessed superhuman strength. Greek mythology might not be as mythical as we think.

Probably the best known offspring of the Nephilim is Goliath. [I. Sam. 17] There is not much written about them, but for a little bit of information, let's turn to Num. 13:27. Now all of the passages that I will use describe the second influx of the giants. The first influx were destroyed in the flood.

I Sam. 13:27 And they told him, and said, We came unto the land whither thou sentest us, and surely it floweth with milk and honey; and this is the fruit of it. 28) Nevertheless the people be strong that dwell in the land, and very great: and moreover we saw the children of ANAK there. [Deut. 1:28] *29) The Amalekites dwell in the land of the south: and the Hittites, and the Jebusites, and the Armorites, dwell in the mountains: and the Canaanites dwell by the sea, and by the coast of Jordan. 30) And Caleb stilled the people before Moses, and said, Let us go up at once, and possess it; for we are well able to overcome it.*

31) But the men that went up with him said, We be not able to go up against the people; for they are stronger than we. 32) And they brought up an evil report of the land which they had searched unto the children of Israel, saying, The land, through which we have gone to search it, is a land that eateth _(destroys) *up the inhabitants thereof; and all the people that we saw in it are men of a great stature. 33) And there we saw the giants, the sons of Anak, which come of the giants: and we were in our own sight as grasshoppers, and so we were in their sight.*

As we just read, there are many different tribes that these Nephilim inter-mixed with. Most of the names end in "ites" format: Kenites, Canaanites, Hittites, Perizzites, Amorites, Girashites, Jebusites, and so on.

For more verses on these giants, look up the word giant in your Strong's Exhaustive Concordance. It will tell you all the verses which contain the word giant.

Now there are also other names that the giants were called. If you turn to *Gen. 14:5) And in the fourteenth year came Chedorlaomer, and the kings that were with him, and smote the REPHAIMS in Ashteroth Karnaim, and the ZUZIMS in Ham, and the EMIMS in Shaveh Kiriathaim.* Also in *Deut.2:10* we read, *The Emims dwelt therein in times past, a people great, and many,* and tall, as the ANAKIMS; 11) Which also were accounted giants, as the Anakims; but the Moabites called them Emims. 12) The HORIMS also dwelt in Seir beforetime; but the children of Esau succeeded them, when they had destroyed them from before they, and dwelt in their stead; as Israel did unto the land of his possession, which the Lord gave unto them.

Just like the tribes with their names ending in "ites", most of the Rephaim names and tribes ended in "ims". So when you come across a name ending in "ites" or "ims", it's a good chance they are enemies of God and Israel.

I would also like to mention that if a name ends in "el" this also is good chance that they are of God. Abel, Gabriel, Michael, Israel, and so on.

Now getting back to the Nephilim. All through much of the Old Testament, Yahveh commands Israel [His chosen people] to completely destroy these wicked tribes. And not just kill the inhabitants, but destroy livestock, buildings, idols, and of course, the women and children. Yahveh did not want the offspring of the Nephilim to continue.

This is why Yahveh was about to send The Great Deluge. Gen.6:5 say's And God saw that the wickedness of man was great in the earth, and that every imagination of the thoughts of his heart (mind) was only evil continually. 6) And it repented the Lord that he had made man on the earth, and it grieved him at his heart.

Now, what was going on you ask? Why was Yahveh so angry at man? Well let's turn to Matt. 24:37 But as the days of Noah were, so shall the coming of the Son of man be. 38) For as in the days that were before the flood they were eating and drinking, *marrying and giving in marriage, until the day that Noah entered into the ark, 39) And knew not until the flood came, and* **TOOK THEM ALL AWAY***; so shall also the* **COMING OF THE SON OF MAN BE.**

Now there is much information contained in these verses. First of all, at the time of the flood, the people were party maniacs. Eating, drinking, orgies, and because of lawlessness, a good chance of thief, killings, and murders. Now these people were Yahveh's chosen people. How many times has this happened.

All through the Bible, you can read about such behavior. Yahveh blesses them and they abuse the freedoms. They turn something good into something evil. The Nephilim surely contributed to their fall at this time, but still, men and their nations continue to fall into the same old iniquities. The Exodus of God's people from Egypt, Sodom and Gomorrah, America. (just another little joke.) **(Not!)** Well anyway, at the time of the flood, all of Yahveh's people, or at least, the generations of Adam, had succumb to partaking in sin; well, almost everyone.

We read in *Gen.6:8 But Noah found grace in the eyes of the Lord. 9) These are the generations of Noah: Noah was a just man and* **PERFECT** *in his* **GENERATIONS***, and Noah walked with God.*

What the word perfect means is that Noah did not intermix with the Nephilim or their offspring. Noah was the last man on earth to still have the perfect pedigree of Adam. All others had; in one way or another, mixed with the Nephilim, the offspring of the Nephilim, or one of the sixth day races of people.

[I would like to say that there is nothing wrong with interracial marriage. It just was not in God's plan at this time.]

This is the reason Yahveh chose Noah to build an ark. Verse 13 say's, *And God said unto Noah, The end of all flesh is come before me; for the earth is filled with violence through them; and behold, I will destroy them* (from) *with the earth.*

Now, as my own personal belief goes, I do not believe the flood was world wide. The flood was to destroy only the Nephilim, their offspring, and all others that partook of the evils around them.

I'd like to say that Noah's situation, is the same as the one for Sodom and Gomorrah. Just as Lot and his family escaped the consuming fire, so does Noah and his family escape the great flood.

Everyone left behind deserved death. As it says in *Rom.6:23 For the wages of sin is death; but the **GIFT** of God is eternal life through Jesus Christ our Lord.*

This is also why I believe we don't live to be 900 years old, as Adam did. Throughout the history of the Bible, man's age slowly continues to decline. By the time we reach Moses, man's age is down to 120.

This is because we are all born into sin and the traditions of them. To live past 120 years today is truly a miracle of God.

We are all born with the sins of our fathers and the fathers before them and the fathers before them. Truly, most of today's humans do not deserve to live past 120.

If you take the average man, most of his sins today are normal behavior. Swearing is just one example. I know some people that every second word out of their mouth is a cuss word. Another example is when you talk bad about someone. If you say something like, I don't like Joe because he always wears the same clothes, or Judy will never amount to anything, you are committing a sin because you have just murdered that person's name. That is what talking bad about someone is called. You are murdering their name. A few more examples of acceptable sin are those against our bodies.

Drinking excessively, smoking, overeating, sex without marriage, and so on are all accepted by the majority of people, yet it is still sin. And those sins, as little as they seem, all add up to a shortened life. OK, enough about why we don't live to be 900 years old, let's get back to Noah.

Like I said before, I don't believe the flood was world wide. It was only for the area in which the Nephilim dwelt. I once saw a picture. I wish I had it to show you, but the picture was of the land where Noah lived. And this area was surrounded by mountains.

Verse *7:20* say's, *Fifteen cubits upward did the waters prevail; and the mountains were covered.*

I truly feel that the waters completely filled the huge valley, and at the end of the flood, spilled over the tops of the mountains.

There are old Chinese writings that speak of a flood, but they themselves, were not flooded out. There are also writings from other civilizations saying the same thing. Now if I am wrong about the flood, the only explanation that must be agreed on is that Noah and his family were not the only people in the ark.

In verse *7:15* it say's, *And they went in unto Noah into the ark, two and two OF ALL FLESH, wherein is the breath of life.*

If the flood was world wide, and if all human life outside the ark was destroyed, then a pair of people from every race created on the sixth day, had to be in the ark also. Some use the excuse that maybe Noah's sons had wives of the other races. This is totally false.

Yahveh at this time wanted all races kept pure. I will not except the theory that all Black people, or say, Chinese people, or any other race came from the generations of Noah and his sons.

There was either a pair of each race in the ark, or the flood was not world wide. That's the only two answers we can accept as true.

So the choice is yours. The flood was world wide, or the flood was only in the land where the Nephilim dwelt. My personal belief is a partial flooding of the earth. Either way it truly doesn't matter.

OUR SALVATION IS IN JESUS, and not on how the flood occurred.

Well we're getting close to the end here. Chapter 8, the flood comes to an end. Verse 20, the first altar is made by Noah and he praises the Lord with burnt offerings. Which by the way, we don't have to do anymore, because Yahshua is that offering today.

So when the new temple is built in the middle east, and animal sacrifices start up again, don't be pulled into the abominations.

Verse 22 tells us that the seasons shall not come to an end, which also tells us there will not be a nuclear war.

Chapter 9 verse 2 tells us that we are responsible for the preservation of all animal life on the earth. Verses 5 and 6, we are responsible for sending murderers back to the Lord. [If you read the capital punishment comment on page 73 then you already know how I feel.] Verses 11-17 Yahveh establishes a covenant with us never to flood the earth as He did. And for a sign of this promise, He gives us the rainbow. Verse 22 we have the mention of **THE NAKEDNESS OF HIS FATHER**, [That information is on page 80.] And after that we have chapter 10, the generations of Noah which brings us to a close of the book, **GENESIS: A CLOSER LOOK.**

PART SIX: GENESIS: A CLOSER LOOK. THE WHOLE PICTURE

In this last chapter, we're going to recap Genesis for a complete picture of understanding. You can say that this is the cheater chapter.

Now, before anything came into existence, God existed. No dust, no molecules, not even an atom. Yahveh is the beginning, and He will be there at the very end.

The first of His creations were millions upon millions of Angels. He called these beings "His children." They were created perfect as He was, without sin, and with a spirit composed body. Yahveh created them for His own pleasure and enjoyment.

The next of His creations were the planets, stars, and a never ending universe. As He brought the heavens into existence, His children sang with joy. One of the planets created was Earth, and on this planet all of Yahveh's children enjoyed a life too perfect and beautiful for our minds to truly understand.

The throne of Yahveh was protected by Cherubims, one of which was named Lucifer. He was perfect and the most beautiful Cherub of all. But because of his beauty and perfection, Lucifer's mind and actions became corrupt, violent, and greedy.

Never repenting or asking forgiveness for the multitude of his sins, Lucifer seduced one third of God's children into following him.

Rebelling against Yahveh, Lucifer declared war against God, but he failed to overtake the throne.

Because of this rebellion, Yahveh destroyed all life on the earth with a flood and threw the heavens into total darkness. The only forms of life remaining were the children of God, which included the rebels and Yahveh himself. This was the demise of the world that then was, as written in II Peter 3:5-7.

For better understanding, I call this point of time: the **FIRST WORLD AGE**.

Yahveh's next step was to decide what to do with Lucifer and his followers. He decided to sentence Lucifer to destruction, and he will be destroyed at the end of the **THIRD WORLD AGE**. [the Millennium]

As for all the others, a plan of repentance and salvation was put into action. This segment of time is called: the heavens and earth which are now, or the **SECOND WORLD AGE**.

The plan starts out with the heavens and earth being restored with light and the earth again is filled with an abundance of plant and animal life. As for the children of God, all of them would have to go through a life on earth entombed in a body which consists of flesh and blood. This experience would prove once and for all, how terrible life away from God really is.

This plan would not only bring some of the rebellious children back, but it could also weed out some that didn't rebel in the First World Age but might of if they were given more time.

Living a life not knowing if God exists could very easily turn good into bad. The whole point is for Yahveh's children to have a free will, and with that free will to still want to live side by side with Him. Yahveh loves us so much that His plan is cut and dry.

After the Third World Age passes, all those remaining will positively; and with a free will; want eternal life in His kingdom.

OK, so we have Yahveh restoring the earth and filling it with all kinds of plant and animal life. All of which; by the way,

MULTIPLIES AFTER ITSELF! Evolution is a false belief. Things do evolve, but not to the extent of man from ameba.

On the sixth day, Yahveh creates mankind. Male and female of all the different races this world has.

On the seventh day, Yahveh watches over and admirers all of His achievement.

Now the earth had hunters and fishermen, but it did not have a man to till the ground. There were no farmers. So on the eighth day, Yahveh formed from the dust of the earth; the man named Adam. This was the creation of the Adamic race.

Also formed were the domesticated farm animals, of which Adam named.

Now the reason Yahveh took special interest in Adam, was not because He loved him more, or that Adam deserved such blessings. It was simply that Yahshua, [Yahveh in a flesh and blood body] would be born in a future generation of his. Adam was the start of the so called, chosen people. And that's the only reason they're called the chosen people. They're not blessed any more than you and I. We are all equal in the eyes of God. The blessings come depending on how you live your life, and if you truly believe Yahveh is the living God and that He became flesh and died for your sins.

The chosen people were blessed because they knew He was the true God, and they; most of the time, kept His laws. That is how you get the blessings of God. No matter what your race, you too can be one of God's chosen by keeping His ways and doing what's right.

We're going to continue on with Adam. Now Yahveh did take special interest in him and our Bibles tell the history of these people, but like I said, he was no better then you or me. And for the proof we go to the garden where Adam was formed.

Now Yahveh took from Adam a chuck of flesh and bone and formed Eve; Adam's counterpart. OK, so we have the sixth day races multiplying on the earth, we have Adam and Eve in the garden of Eden, we have Yahshua as the tree of life, and we have Lucifer as the tree with the knowledge of good and evil.

Now there was only one rule to follow, do not eat (Partake) of the fruit of the tree with the knowledge of good and evil, so what do you think they did? They ate an apple right? **WRONG!**

All our lives we have believed, and told our children, that Adam and Eve ate an apple. This is a lie. Now I can't really blame my parents, or their parents, or even the parents before them. In *Dan. 12:8* Daniel asks the Lord, *What shall be the end of all these things? And the Lord said, Go thy way Daniel: for the words are closed up and sealed till the time of the end.*[end of the 2nd world age, which is now] *10) Many shall be purified, and made white, and tried; but the wicked* (one) *shall do wickedly: and none of the wicked shall understand; but the wise shall understand.* (God's word)

I will not put the blame on my passed generations for not knowing the truth about the garden of Eden. Yahveh tells us that He hid the truth. What happened in the garden is just like the parables Yahshua told to the multitudes. It wasn't for them to understand. But it is important to us today.

As a matter of fact, it is very important to know the truth of God's word today.

One reason being, since these are the last days and the return of Yahshua is at the door, Yahveh said He would pour out His knowledge. The Bible has been unsealed. Yahveh wants this end of the age generation to know the truth. Many strange things are going to take place, and if you don't know where to turn or which way to go, you'll be in a lot of trouble, and a world of hurt. Chances are, you'll end up following the false Christ, the anti-Christ. And if you're a believer of the rapture, you're headed for a big disappointment, because it's not going to happen. At least, not the way you think it is.

I'm not going to get into it right now, but believe me, the rapture is just another lie set up by Satan to deceive and destroy.

OK, let's get back to Adam and Eve, and what happened in the garden.

Well to get right to the point, the serpent; which of course is Lucifer, seduced Eve into having sexual intercourse. Many will say that I'm crazy, but if you read all the information included in this book, or read your Bible properly, it's a proven fact. A sexual affair did take place.

Now I am not going to go over it again, so we'll just continue on. Chapter four we have the birth of Cain and Abel, which were fraternal twins. Lucifer was the father of Cain, and Adam was the father of Abel.

The end of chapter four we have Cain's generations. His family and the generations that followed are known as Kenites, or sons of Cain. Chapter five we have the generations of Adam up till the time of Noah and his sons.

Starting chapter six we have the reason Yahveh sends the great flood. As Adam's family grew, Lucifer and his followers; left the heavens; and against Yahveh's plan, come down to the earth and had sexual intercourse with any woman they wanted. The plan of Yahveh's was to have every spirit being to be born of woman and be placed into a flesh and blood body. Why? To experience one human lifetime. But these fallen angels couldn't wait and against God's plan, came down from heaven and started reproducing children on earth.

Now I would like to mention that the fallen angels that came down from heaven, only numbered 7,000. [Rev.11:13]

Lucifer did deceive one third of all angels in the first world age, but there was only 7,000 that left their place in heaven to come down to earth and had intercourse with women. [Jude, 6]

So now we come to the flood of Noah. The reason Yahveh sends the flood, is to destroy all the offspring that the fallen angels produced. They are mentioned in our Bibles as giants. There are also many who believe that Greek mythology; are in fact, these giant offspring.

Also it's a good chance these giants were used to build the great pyramids. But there is no proof of this information.

So, Yahveh sends the flood; which by the way, I feel was not world wide, and destroys the giants. But even after the flood there were still some around. The best known is Goliath. I don't know if some of them lived through the flood, or if the same thing happened again with the angels coming down to earth, but they were still around.

Well, I hate to say it, but we're pretty much at the end of this book. Covering Genesis chapters one through ten, the flood is probably the last big event.

There is however; in chapter nine verses 18 to 27, the Nakedness of his Father. It's covered on page 80 if you haven't read it yet. But otherwise, this reading is coming to an end. I hope you enjoyed the book;

GENESIS: A CLOSER LOOK.

My reason for writing it was to inform you on all the misconceptions we all grew up with. The Bible is not a book of stories. It's a message from God telling us about the passed, the present, and the future. Why we're here and where we're going.

Mysteries of the Bible that have boggled man's mind can now be answered. And the only reason why we understand now, is because **THESE ARE THE LAST DAYS**. The return of Yahshua will happen in this generation. I will not set a date, but all the signs my Bible tells me to look for are here. It's a wonder to me how someone cannot believe in a living God. The proof is everywhere if you would just take the time to open up your spiritual eyes and ears.

Well, like I said before, I hoped you enjoyed this book and all it's knowledge and information. None of us are perfect; including me. But I personally feel that the information contained in this book is 90% accurate and true. We all have our own thoughts and beliefs, but as I always say, truth is truth. You can't change it, you can't manipulate it. It's what I diligently seek and constantly strive for.

The only way anyone can be 100% true in wisdom and knowledge is to die. And that's not in my plans right now. I hope it's not in yours either.

Again, I would like to say,
may Yahveh bless you, your family and your friends.
And enjoy your personal search for the truth.

Notes

Notes

Favorite Verses

ABBREVIATIONS

(Old Testament)

Gen . . . . Genesis	Eccl . . . . Ecclesiastes
Ex . . . . Exodus	Song . . . . . Song of Solomon
Lev. . . . . Leviticus	Is . . . . Isaiah
Num . . . . Numbers	Jer. . . . . Jeremiah
Deut . . . . . . Deuteronomy	Lam . . . . Lamenations
Josh . . . . Joshua	Eze . . . . Ezekiel
Judg . . . . Judges	Dan . . . . Daniel
Ruth. . . . . Ruth	Hos . . . . Hosea
1Sa . . . . 1 Samuel	Joel . . . . Joel
2Sa . . . . 2 Samuel	Amos. . . . . Amos
1Kin. . . . . 1 Kings	Obad. . . . . Obadiah
2Kin. . . . . 2 Kings	Jonah . . . . Jonah
1Chr. . . . . . . 1 Chronicles	Mic. . . . . Micah
2Chr. . . . . . . 2 Chronicles	Nah. . . . . Nahum
Ezr . . . . Ezra	Hab . . . . Habakkuk
Neh . . . . Nehemiah	Zeph . . . . Zephaniah
Est . . . . Esther	Hag . . . . Haggai
Job . . . . Job	Zec . . . . Zechariah
Ps. . . . . Psalms	Mal . . . . Malachi
Prov . . . . Proverbs	

(New Testament)

Mt. . . . . Matthew	1Ti . . . . 1 Timothy
Mk . . . . Mark	2Ti . . . . 2 Timothy
Lk . . . . Luke	Titus . . . . Titus
Jn . . . . John	Philem. . . . . Philemon
Acts . . . . Acts	Heb . . . . Hebrews
Rom . . . . Romans	Jas . . . . James
1Cor . . . . . . 1 Corinthians	1Pet . . . . 1 Peter
2Cor . . . . . . 2 Corinthians	2Pet . . . . 2 Peter
Gal. . . . . Galatians	1Jn . . . . 1 John
Eph . . . . Ephesians	2Jn . . . . 2 John
Phil . . . . Philippians	3Jn . . . . 3 John
Col . . . . Colossians	Jude. . . . . Jude
1Th . . . . . 1 Thessalonians	Rev. . . . . Revelation
2Th . . . . . 2 Thesalonians	

SCRIPTURE VERSES IN THE ORDER OF APPEARANCE

SCRIPTURE VERSES IN THE ORDER OF APPEARANCE

SCRIPTURE VERSES IN ORDER BY BOOK
(Old Testament)

SCRIPTURE VERSES IN ORDER BY BOOK
(New Testament)

About the Cover

Born in Caprese, Tuscany 4:30 am, 3/6/1475, Michelangelo Buonarroti would become the greatest artistic genius of all time. His imperishable work in sculpture, painting, arch. and poetry put him far and above all other artists to date. In the Autumn of 1474, 30 year old Lodovico Buonarri had the gratifying news that he was appointed to a six month term as Gov. of Chiusi and Caprese, two small towns 40 miles from Florence. Lodovico left Florence on horseback with his 19 year old wife, Francesca Miniato, and their first born Lionardo who was 1-½ years old at the time.

Taking residence in an old, partially ruined castle high above the Tiber River, Francesca, six months later, gave birth to Michelangelo, the second of five sons. Lodovico's term of office ended, and with the family's newest addition, returned to Caprese. At this time Francesca found herself unable to nurse the baby, who consequently was sent to Settignano to stay with a wet nurse and her husband.

This region had many quarries, and like most of the men there, the nurse's husband worked as a stone cutter. Here stonecutting was not merely a livelihood but a normal way of life. And it was this life Michelangelo consumed. He never really returned to the house of his father; always feeling insecure and tentative, mainly because of his mother's failing health, and his father's endless demands, complaints, and the need for more children. At age 6, Angelo's mother, Francesca, died. She was a only 25 years old. Afterward, Angelo lived 4 more years as the son of the stonecutter and his wife, only occasionally visiting his father. At this time, Angelo could not read or write, but was very skillful with the hammer and chisel. At the age of 10 he was confronted for the first time with school, and for the next 3 years Angelo learned to read and write, but not much more. He did, however, love to sketch and draw and at the age of 13, Angelo's best friend, Francesca Granacci, an apprentice in the workshop of Domenico Ghirlandaio, the cities best, convinced Angelo into leaving school and become an artist. This outraged his father who wanted all his sons in government or trade. To be an artist in Lodovico's mind was no more glamourous than a construction/labor worker.

With malicious and cold hearted intentions, Lodovico wrote up a public "Bill of Sale" stating that his son would stay for 3 years studying under the Grand Masters, Domenico and David de Tommaso, the art of painting, thus sending Michelangelo on his way into artistic history. The masterpiece of Angelo's youth was the *Pietá* (1499), today a treasure of St. Peter's in Rome. It shows a crucified Yahshua in the arms of Madonna. Two years later he produced the *Bruges Madonna* or better known as Madonna with child. And in 1501, Michelangelo started work on his greatest stone work ever, the 17' fall Statue of David. Finished in 1504, it's probably the most popular known statue to date.

About the Cover

I always wondered how Yahveh formed Adam from the dust of the ground, and after seeing the stone work of Michelangelo, I wonder no more. Who knows, maybe Michelangelo was Melchisedec also, - or just maybe, he was Micheal the Arch-Angel, now there's something to think about.

In 1508, the 33 year old was hired by Uncle Julius Sixtus IV to start his most powerful work ever: The Sistine Chapel. Built in 1473 for Julius Sixtus IV whose name it bears, was made with two functions in mind: The 1st a private chapel of the Popes, and 2nd for defense against attack. The chapel is 132' x 44' with a ceiling 68' above a marble mosaic floor. The brick walls are 3' thick with high windows and a narrow entrance, thus making it difficult to invade. Battlements on the roof, and quarters for soldiers above the vault made it a fortress-refuge. Here Angelo had 5,800 sq. feet to work with. Although the original plan called for only 12 figures, Michelangelo painted over 350 figures. The greatest known plate is: the Creation of Adam. Yahveh is shown bringing Adam to Life with **HIS TOUCH**, and in his arm is Eve looking on with excited eyes.

Above this plate is the creation of Eve, where you can see Adam's limp body at rest. The next plate is: The Fall of Man. Here the serpent; depicted as a woman, is the tree of Good & Evil, with the left side of the tree temptation, and on the right side, expulsion from the garden. Two plates further is: The Drunkenness of Noah. Here Noah's sons are covering his naked body as written in Gen. 9:22, but this plate is mistranslated by Angelo and as you have learned for yourself, the nakedness of Noah has nothing to do with him being naked. [p. 80] Painting on a scaffold by himself, it took 4 years to complete the ceiling. Afterwards he took care of other projects, but was ordered back to the chapel in 1535 to paint the front wall, better known as: The Last Judgement. At the age of 61, it took Angelo 5 years to complete. Unveiled in 1541, the Last Judgement is an awe-inspiring masterpiece. It was to represent humanity face to face with salvation.

Michelangelo's own life ended on 7/18/1564. He said that "Life should be a journey from the inslaved body to the liberation of the Spirit in God." His work set him apart from all others, and he achieved this by bringing the Bible to life through his artistic genius. Thank you Michelangelo for your dedication, devotion and Love of God.

Truth Publications

The RETURN of YAHSHUA

Let no man deceive you by any means: for that day shall not come, except there come a falling away first, and that man of sin be revealed, the son of Perdition,

II Thes 2:3

And the great dragon was cast out, that old serpent, which deceiveth the whole world: he was cast out into the earth, and his angels were cast out with him.

Rev. 12:9

And I saw an angel come down from heaven, having the key of the bottomless pit and a great chain in his hand. And he laid hold on the dragon, that old serpent, which is the Devil, and Satan, and bound him a 1,000 years [mill.] and cast him into the bottomless pit, and shut him up, and set a seal upon him, that he should deceive the nations no more, till the 1,000 years should be fulfilled; and after that he must be loosed a little season.

Rev. 20:1-3

For the Lord himself shall descend from heaven with a shout, with the voice of the archangel, and with the trump of God: and the dead in Christ shall rise first: then we which are alive and remain shall be caught up together with them in clouds (groups, gatherings) to meet the Lord in air: (spirit body) and so shall we ever be with the Lord.

I Thes. 4:16, 17

And death and hell were cast into the Lake of Fire, this is the second death. (of the soul and spirit) And whosoever was not found written in the Book of Life was cast into the Lake of Fire.

Rev. 20:14, 15

And, behold, I come quickly; and my reward is with me, to give every man according as his work shall be. I am Alpha and Omega, the beginning and the end, the first and the last.

Rev. 22:12, 13